Breakthrough
Triathlon
Training

BRAD KEARNS

McGraw·Hill

New York   Chicago   San Francisco   Lisbon   London   Madrid   Mexico City
Milan   New Delhi   San Juan   Seoul   Singapore   Sydney   Toronto

Library of Congress Cataloging-in-Publication Data

Kearns, Brad, 1965–
      Breakthrough triathlon training / Brad Kearns.— 1st ed.
            p.   cm.
      ISBN 0-07-146279-1
      1. Triathlon—Training.   I. Title.

      GV1060.73.K43   2006
      796.42'57—dc22   2005017241

1 2 3 4 5 6 7 8 9 0   DOC/DOC   0 9 8 7 6 5

ISBN 0-07-146279-1

McGraw-Hill books are available at special quantity discounts to use as premiums and sales promotions, or for use in corporate training programs. For more information, please write to the Director of Special Sales, Professional Publishing, McGraw-Hill, Two Penn Plaza, New York, NY 10121-2298. Or contact your local bookstore.

This book is printed on acid-free paper.

CONTENTS

Contents

Part 2 Training Principles and Strategy

PART 3 DEVELOPING THE MIND OF
        A CHAMPION

FOREWORD

I have known Brad Kearns since 1987, when he was an established pro triathlete and I was a 15-year-old kid jumping into races on the pro circuit and beginning my journey as a professional athlete. I must say Brad is different—he's a trip! Most athletes I have trained and competed with over the years are focused on themselves, their training, their equipment, and beating the competition. Brad always had a different perspective, looking at a bigger picture of athletics and the lifestyle of a professional athlete.

My rapid rise to the top of the cycling world, followed by my ordeal with cancer and subsequent comeback to professional cycling, was a journey that matured me quickly and broadened my perspective. Quite honestly, as a young athlete I was motivated primarily by money. I grew to understand that there are deeper motivations for being an athlete that are more powerful and rewarding than just the rush of winning and the superficial rewards it brings.

I've always known this deep down, and I think this is true for everyone competing in endurance sports. Brad's perspective, captured eloquently and often humorously in this book, can serve as a wake-up call for a healthy mind-set and a mature, sincere approach to your athletic career. You don't find this type of book too often among the selections for endurance athletes.

There are plenty of books about training methods, technique instruction, and competitive strategies, and these elements are crucial to your success. To be a champion requires a comprehensive approach where nothing is left to chance or dismissed as immaterial. People tease me for obsessing over my bike equipment, double- and triple-checking the race route, or focusing intently on heart rates and wattage output during training sessions. This might seem a little overboard for the casual observer, but I am committed to doing my sport correctly and giving my absolute best performance in competition.

While this stuff is all critical to my success, I think my mind-set could be an even more powerful advantage over my competition. The reason I am so passionate about every element of my cycling career is because I love it. I love my job, my lifestyle, the interaction with my teammates, and the compelling goal of winning the Tour de France. If I didn't (which unfortunately is the case with many athletes), I could not will myself to care so much and prepare so intently.

Breakthrough Triathlon Training will help you connect with that deep love of the sport that can be your greatest weapon for success. As I relate in my books *It's Not About the Bike* and *Every Second Counts*, I have had the good fortune to be influenced by teammates, friends, family members, and people in the cancer community who help connect me with a higher purpose for competing in cycling. After you finish this book, I hope you will add it to the list of positive and powerful influences in your athletic career.

—Lance Armstrong

Brad Kearns autographs his book for a big fan.

CREDIT: SHANNON HANEL

ACKNOWLEDGMENTS

I have been supported by a tremendous group of family and friends in all my endeavors, even when they were wild and wacky. My parents Walter and Gail barely blinked when I announced that I was quitting my respectable job at the world's largest accounting firm (after 11 weeks on the payroll) to try my luck on the pro triathlon circuit. My wife Tracy has offered unconditional love and support on the roller-coaster journey that was my nine-year career as a professional triathlete and has continued after I quit racing. It's not easy to keep your head straight when you are immersed in an intense game like competing as a professional athlete, and I was very fortunate that my family helped me keep a healthy perspective at all times.

My many training partners and counterparts on the pro circuit were of course central to my experience. We all can take credit for pushing each other to the outer limits of human endurance performance, and for laying the foundation and the performance standards for athletes in the future to thrive. Andrew MacNaughton was there from the beginning. I learned more from him than from anyone else, for he knows more than anyone else. We gave each other the courage to train harder than we were supposed to and to break the monopoly that the top athletes had on breaking the finish tape. It would be unfathomable to have attempted or achieved this alone.

Thanks also to Farley Chase of Waxman Group and Mark Weinstein of McGraw-Hill for making this book a reality; photographers Liz Kreutz and Lois Schwartz; Johnny G for peeling the orange; Jonathan Mello, Willie J, and BK for the plane ride; Mark Sisson for

Acknowledgments

inventing Bricks and Key Workouts; Dr. Dave Kobrine for seven points in nine seconds; Steve Kobrine for the 5 A.M. car pool; Steve Dietch for demonstrating how to suffer at a young age without food, water, or slowing down; Robert Benun for being the second-best athlete at Collier; Andy and Tam Robles for the sizzled ahi; Kevin Pedrotti for the cell phone; Edge for being unstoppable; Jim Northey for the Otis muffins; Bob Powers for the Square D car; Kerry Dunigan for the cycling tips; Mary Ann and Bern Dunigan for Indian food in Paris; Neil Kearns for the gold coin; Wally Kearns for the seat cushion at Dodger Stadium; Jeff Kearns for the high-five at The OC; Katie Kearns for spacing on her homework; and Jack and Maria for the chalk world.

INTRODUCTION

"Results happen naturally when motivation is pure."

This sentence summarizes the most important lesson I learned in my nine years competing as a professional triathlete. I believe it is the key to your success and enjoyment of the sport. Having a pure motivation means doing the sport for the love of training and competition, to learn and grow as a person through athletic challenges, and to promote a healthy, fit lifestyle. When you are driven by these higher ideals—instead of more superficial motivations—you are able to unlock some attractive doors. Cultivating a pure motivation will help you enjoy performance breakthroughs far beyond current levels; experience less stress, tension, and anxiety related to competition; experience less fatigue from your training regimen; and enjoy your athletics on a deeper level than ever before.

Breakthrough Triathlon Training will take you on a journey that covers every aspect of your training, competition, and enjoyment of a triathlon and of a healthy, fit lifestyle. In contrast, almost all of the books and magazine articles about triathlons cover only a single dimension of peak performance—physical training. While it is very beneficial to learn about workout theory and application, competitive strategies, cool equipment, and proper technique, the physical element is only one piece of the pie. Because your triathlon career exists inside of a bigger picture called daily life, your approach must be *holistic*—encompass the whole picture—to generate results and enjoyment.

A champion athlete is someone who is skilled and balanced not only physically but mentally and emotionally. Champion athletes train and race extremely hard, but they also have a tremendous ability to back off when they need to, stay positive after defeat and disappointment, and be flexible in their thoughts and actions. They have an honest and sincere commitment to their peak performance goals that is more powerful than ego demands, personal insecurities, and the lure of the unhealthy, sedentary modern world. Champions are able to maintain physical, mental, and emotional health in pursuit of fitness. Watching the champion on the racecourse is a tip-of-the-iceberg glimpse of a comprehensive peak performance operation. Being a champion requires the devoted application of many talents and disciplines behind the scenes every single day.

My approach will help you learn and implement these broad abilities into your triathlon game plan. In doing so, you will break free of the one-dimensional, robotic approach favored by many athletes. It seems most of the focus in our sport is on the accumulation of physical work and competitive results, where nothing matters more than the numbers in the logbook or on the finish line clock. The instant gratification and ego boost of dropping training partners on a bike ride seems to be enough of a payoff that we forget to aspire to anything deeper from our athletic experience. It's like the Hollywood movies that play to the lowest common denominator; sex and violence will always be an easier sell than the film festival flicks that force you to think.

Often in my professional career I succumbed to the pressures of the rat race and developed an unhealthy obsession with results. When I drifted away from a natural, balanced, intuitive training approach and became too focused, driven, and obsessive, my training and performance suffered. Many times I fell into a tailspin of fatigue and poor performance as a result of getting overly wound up in my career as a pro jock. I would search outside of myself for answers when all I really needed to succeed was to cultivate my intuition and pursue a healthy, balanced lifestyle. When I was able to get over myself, get out of my own way, and let the process of fitness happen naturally, I enjoyed peak performance.

Consequently, the approach I advocate is simple and refreshing. It is not a matter of learning a bunch of new, top-secret training concepts and mental toughness mind games. It's more a matter of getting out of your own way—relaxing the mind and body, going with the natural flow of fitness progress, and enjoying every moment of your experience.

In Part 1, I will discuss attitude and philosophical approach. You will learn the power of pure motivation and how to discard the superficial and often destructive elements of the rat race—obsessive behavior, ego-driven actions, or anything that is imbalanced or unhealthy relating to your approach to the sport. You will learn why triathletes suffer too much in training and competition and collectively perform far below their potential. You will discover an alternative approach to training where you are guided by intuition instead of ego demands and external pressure.

In Part 2, I will get into the nuts and bolts of how to train your body properly for peak performance. You will learn the basic training principles like periodization and aerobic base building that have been proven effective by 40 years of competitive results from the world's greatest endurance athletes—but are blatantly ignored and abused by many triathletes. You will go behind the scenes and discover the secrets of the training regimens of some of the top endurance athletes of all time, gleaning insights into what to do and what *not* to do.

You will learn how to design effective weekly, monthly, and annual training schedules, integrating the proper principles to ensure uninterrupted improvement in your fitness level. You will give every single workout you conduct a specific purpose and avoid the burnout that plagues so many misguided athletes. I will also dispel some of the popular, but flawed, training theories that pervade the sport about swimming, strength training, speed work, and acclimatization—myths that confuse and distract triathletes from their true priorities and prevent them from getting the most bang for their training buck.

My hope is that by the time you finish this journey, you will have totally transformed your approach to the sport. The excitement and inspiration you will feel and the behavior changes you will implement will be infectious. Family and loved ones will no longer be able to complain about the fallout from hanging with the stereotypical triathlete who is too tired to do the chores; who is obsessed with equipment, workouts, food, and sleep; and whose moods fluctuate according to fitness level and age group placings.

Your training partners will see you take the initiative to transform the group dynamics from competitive to complementary. You will be the catalyst in peeling away the insecurity, surreptitious competition, ego battles, general BS, and other unhealthy peer influences that occur when you place a highly motivated group of people together. Instead you will move the emphasis to fun and the camaraderie of working toward a common goal, where it rightfully belongs.

While sharpening up your "good sport" qualities is admirable, let's not forget another benefit of my approach that may interest you: you will race faster! That's right: when you are able to adopt a relaxed and fun-loving approach to the sport, your competitive performances will improve along with your enjoyment of the sport. This may seem like a paradox, for as sports fans we are conditioned to the charade that the most intense, aggressive competitors are the ones who come out ahead. Yes, you need these qualities to succeed as an athlete, but it's important to understand how being a tough competitor integrates into the healthy, balanced lifestyle approach of this book.

When you are good to your body, protect your health while pursuing your fitness, and cultivate a pure motivation, your "eye of the tiger" characteristics will come to the surface naturally when you need them the most—in the heat of a challenging competition.

If you fail to see the bigger picture and bulldoze through your life and athletic career with aggression and an intense need to prove yourself at the forefront, you are bound to struggle in many ways. It's no secret that athletes in the major sports, where the desperate need to win at all costs dwarfs more admirable elements of sport, struggle morally, ethically, and psychologically. Stories about crime, drugs, greed, violence, and poor sportsmanship are concentrated so heavily in the sports pages that it is ridiculous.

You may not be in danger of inciting a riot with fans at the finish line of your next triathlon or dropping dead from an overdose of EPO

xv

Brad Kearns runs his way to a win at the 1990 Orange County Performing Arts Center Triathlon.

CREDIT: LOIS SCHWARTZ

(the frequently abused drug for boosting red blood cells), but an impure approach to your sport will drain your energy, stifle the pure joy of training and racing, and make an already hard sport seem even more difficult.

I've personally seen many other athletes discard the pressures of the rat race in favor of a pure and natural training approach with stunning results on the racecourse. I will relate inspirational stories along these lines and also give you a step-by-step process to follow, opening the door for you to experience amazing performance breakthroughs.

PART I

ATTITUDE
AND
PHILOSOPHY

CHAPTER 1

THE POWER OF PURE MOTIVATION

The Genius Athlete

The wonderful thing about athletics is that it can be a vehicle for growth in your life, or it can mirror the attitude and behavior issues that are present in other areas of your life. When your motivation is influenced by the accumulation of results, compulsive drives, ego demands, and peer pressure, you drift away from pure motivation.

I believe this is the typical approach in the triathlon world today. With the tremendous growth of the sport, we see droves of highly motivated, goal-oriented, high-achieving, type-A humans pushing their bodies to exhaustion in search of ego satisfaction and more accomplishments to post on their résumés. While the accomplishments and the miles on the road do pile up, they often come at the expense of a balanced life, family and personal relationships, mental and physical health, true athletic potential, and full enjoyment of the experience.

Because of the personality type attracted to the sport, triathletes often apply the same success formula to athletics as they did to law school or moving up the corporate ladder. This involves results-oriented training methods and belief systems. If it worked building your career, it should work on your body. So you push through adversity and distractions to stubbornly accomplish what you set out to do, constantly measure and judge your performances against your peers or arbitrary benchmarks of time or place, and dictate your happiness and satisfaction by your results. Do this in the business world and you get ahead; not so in the athletic world. The difference between your career and your body is that athletic success depends on a holistic approach—leading a healthy (physically, mentally, and emotionally), balanced lifestyle as you pursue competitive fitness.

When you pursue fitness at the expense of your health or against the laws of nature and balance, you will break down in the form of mediocre performances, injury, illness, burnout, or lack of full enjoyment and appreciation of your athletics. When you force your body to do something it is not naturally meant to do, you will always suffer negative consequences. This is an inexorable law of nature, like gravity or the passing of time. We all know this to be true, so we attempt to avoid this trouble by following a carefully planned training schedule. It's a good start—well-intentioned—but it's not enough.

The problem for today's athlete is not lack of knowledge about training principles or workout ideas. The problem comes when you treat your training schedule as an entity independent from your lifestyle. An effective training schedule must be dynamic and always reflect your lifestyle. This goes against the grain of the compulsive type-A personality, who has a strong desire to control everything in his environment—knowing with certainty how much money he spends and makes, how many weekly miles he plans to ride, and what his pace is for each individual event at the triathlon race.

Your body does not know or comprehend any of these external variables; these are all games for your mind. While your body is ignorant of your event splits or your USA Triathlon federation national ranking, it has other forms of tremendous wisdom, often untapped by today's triathlete. Your body connects with things like energy level, effort level (it reports back to you in the form of heart rate, among other things), and homeostasis (where all systems of the body are functioning normally and in balance). A pain in your knee is a report from your body that homeostasis is not present, that your joint is inflamed. That's all your body knows—it doesn't care whether you are trying to impress your training partners by going off the front during a tough workout, or whether you are on PR (personal record) pace at mile 22 of the marathon; it just knows that your knee hurts.

As author Deepak Chopra discusses in his number one bestseller *Ageless Body, Timeless Mind*, we have wisdom in every cell of our bodies. When we have butterflies in our stomach or a broken heart, it can be quantified on a cellular level by elevated hormone levels, blood pressure and heart rate changes, and so forth. A nervous stomach is a physical, chemical manifestation of what you are thinking, feeling, and doing in your life.

Why is this mind-body mumbo jumbo important to someone who wants to improve her 40K split? Because when you pay attention to something other than your mind, you become a smarter athlete more capable of making the right training decisions that lead to peak performance. For example, when the body sends a signal to your mind in the form of a sore throat or knee pain, you can respect and appreciate the wisdom of your body and make the right choices to return to balance. It might mean that you stop running until your knee pain subsides or cut back on training volume when work or family demands squeeze your time. When your body sends a positive signal with high energy levels and supple, strong muscles firing rhythmically and effortlessly, the mind can become naturally inspired to push toward peak performance.

In addition to your body's physical, cellular wisdom, you also possess a tremendous emotional wisdom—an awareness of your emotional state and how emotions affect everything that you do. This concept was made popular by the bestseller *Emotional Intelligence* by Daniel Goleman. Goleman argues that IQ offers a very narrow definition of intelligence and that emotional intelligence is a far more powerful indicator of leading a happy and successful life. I can think of few things more important to the success of a triathlete than the self-awareness and personal motivation Goleman describes in his definition of emotional intelligence.

To have the self-awareness and motivation to live the life of a champion athlete every day can be considered a form of genius. It's no wonder corporate America constantly feeds employees a stream of athletic analogies: "Come on team, this is a marathon, we need to raise the bar with a full-court press, execute the game plan, and crush the competition with a touchdown in overtime."

Many champion athletes do not know the capital of Mexico, or of Vermont, or even which one is a state and which is a country. Yet the champion athlete is a genius in doing what he sets out to accomplish. In the case of an endurance athlete, accomplishing a peak performance goal often becomes an all-consuming endeavor that affects every area of his life. The champion athlete must choose to get adequate sleep, eat healthy foods instead of enjoy other temptations, back off when the body sends a message to do so, push hard and remain focused through the challenge of long, hard workouts, and get out of bed after an emotionally crushing defeat to train for the next race.

Making the right choices takes someone with awesome physical, emotional, and mental wisdom. The underlying goal of the champion athlete is to have a positive attitude, high motivation levels, intense focus, and a sense of balance in the face of the all-consuming peak performance challenge. In contrast, there are many great physical talents who don't have the emotional wisdom or the mental makeup to become a champion. The reasons are many: poor decision making, inability to harness ego demands and competitive instincts, lack of pure and deep-seated self-confidence, impatience, compulsiveness, lack of self-awareness or dishonest self-analysis, and other destructive personality traits.

The champion is someone who can blend the yin and yang of a killer instinct and brutal training regimen with a softer side of emotional sensitivity, physical awareness, positive attitude, and balanced approach to life. Lance Armstrong morphed from a self-described one-dimensional, money-chasing jock to an enlightened cancer survivor and spokesperson, family man, and far better athlete. This is a perfect example of how the bigger picture factors into your race times.

When your emotional intelligence tells you that something is out of balance in your life—as expressed by lack of motivation or negative emotions like anger, anxiety, or sadness—you must address it and make adjustments. Sometimes it takes an attitude adjustment, a training schedule adjustment, or even a change of venue. In his book *It's Not About the Bike*, Lance recalls how he pondered retirement during a struggling period in his career. He decided to escape from his normal life for a week of intensive training in Boone, North Carolina. Free from the distractions of home and his normal routine, Lance enjoyed an awesome week of training in Boone. At the conclusion of the week, instead of talking retirement, he set his sights on winning his first Tour de France.

Regaining balance doesn't have to be as dramatic as packing up and heading out of town for some new training scenery. Sometimes returning to balance is as simple as downsizing your training schedule until your emotional health and balance return. Sometimes it means changing a destructive behavior pattern, such as removing your watch for workouts or purposely letting training partners outperform you, to break free of unhealthy competitive relationships. Sometimes it could be an honest, impassioned conversation with a coach or training partners that fosters a more nurturing relationship.

As simple as these things sound, this is the area where the majority of triathletes make their most costly mistakes. When you continue to train when you are physically or emotionally out of balance you inflict tremendous damage upon your body, your mind, and your emotions. As I will discuss in "The Mediocrity Epidemic" section in Chapter 3, I believe that many athletes are not able to dig deep for peak performance because they have depleted their deepest stores of energy and willpower from an imbalanced, overstressed approach to training and life.

As any sports fan knows, the ability to "go to the well"—perform far beyond expectations predicted by fitness levels when it counts the most—is a sign of a true champion. It takes mental, physical, and emotional intelligence to preserve your energy stores, moderate your energy expenditure, and sync your efforts in training with the overall level of stress in your life.

For those of you growing frustrated at reading all these reasons to slow down and back off from the hard training that gives you that beloved endorphin buzz, you may be pleased to note that there is a flip side to this principle. When you break free of the prison of the compulsive mind and the attachment of your self-esteem to your performance, a couple of cool things can happen.

First, you can enjoy the rest and relaxation that you deserve, no longer tormented by the anxiety and tension the obsessive mind generates: "If I miss this swim workout I'll lose my feel of the water"; "If I don't hit 250 miles on the bike this week, my ironman training program will regress"; "I really need to lose 10 pounds—I'm so sick of carrying this extra weight."

Second, you can push your body harder and explore peak performance beyond your imagination. When you reject the compulsive training approach and the demands of the ego, you eliminate a self-imposed ceiling on your performances. What ceiling you ask? Well, consider that a symptom of the obsessive-compulsive, ego-driven approach is a desire to measure, judge, and control everything in your environment. This includes the judgment you place on your ability such that if you exceed your perception of peak performance, your mind may not be comfortable with it. The result is often self-sabotage to bring your performance back down to the expected level. Or, never giving yourself a chance for performance breakthrough due to self-limiting beliefs or statements ("I hate hills"; "I freak out in cold water"; "She is so much more talented than me"; "I suck in the heat"; "I usually break down after mile 13").

The sport of golf provides a dramatic example of this principle. It is frighteningly commonplace for golfers of all levels (even PGA Tour pros) who perform beyond their expectations to then regress to the point of returning to normal. For example, a golfer who averages a score of 90 for 18 holes has the ability, on occasion, to shoot a 39 for 9 holes. Typically what happens after an incredible streak like that is the mind begins to analyze, judge, and obsess over the performance to the point of inhibiting future peak performance. The busy mind causes the player to leave the "zone" and return to earth. The player fires a 51 on the back nine to total a plain ol' 90 at the completion of the round. The phenomenon of choking would not exist if we didn't place so much importance on the results.

The converse is also true. When you perform poorly for a sustained period of time, a powerful inner drive often surfaces to will your performances back to respectability. A 90-average golfer who shoots 51 for the first nine will often channel the disgust and frustration into an intense focus for a breakthrough performance on the back nine; 51 + 39 = 90 any way you slice it. It's easy to see an exciting new possibility on the other side of this imaginary barricade of judgment and attachment.

King of the Desert

I began my career as a professional triathlete in 1986, leaving a miserable accounting job to have some fun, travel around on the pro circuit, and devote my life to getting faster as a triathlete. I was passionate about the sport and the lifestyle and committed to improving my fitness in a healthy, natural manner. I lived a quiet, simple life and was overjoyed to be doing something that I loved on the heels of a disastrous entry into the working world.

My performances were promising—in local events I could place in the top five, and in national events I recorded finishes like 23rd, 15th, and 12th. I was happy to be steadily improving and learning about all facets of the sport and the professional game. During that first year, I would daydream about great success, but I was not overly concerned with making money or challenging the top athletes. I was patient with the natural progression of fitness. I pushed my body hard but also rested when it was appropriate. I was appreciative of every workout and every day I was able to pursue a dream career.

If I had reread this description of my attitude and approach five years later, in the midst of a successful pro career, few of the characteristics would apply. When my career heated up, I often found myself caught up in the scene, with elements of my approach job-like and stressful. I would find myself out on the road doing workouts that were more compulsive and unhealthy than purposeful. I would become preoccupied with sponsorship contracts and getting my photo in the magazines. I wore a bathing suit to work, but when my approach was impure I might as well have worn a business suit for the rat race.

One of the most important messages of this book is to resist getting caught up in unhealthy motivation and preserve that "kid in the candy store" mentality about your triathlon pursuits. It is within reach of all of us and often takes just a snap of the fingers to adjust your mentality. It's no different from being out on a swim and suddenly remembering to implement your coach's tip for "high elbows."

The magic of my innocent, joyful approach that first year was evident not only by the smile on my face but by the steady progression of my fitness to world-class level. The big race that I was focusing on and saving up for at the end of the season was the annual

World Long Course Championships in Nice, France, a nationally televised race featuring a two-mile swim in the Mediterranean, a 75-mile bike ride with serious climbing in the French Alps, and a 20-mile run along the coast and the Promenade des Anglais boardwalk.

My training partner and travel companion was Andrew Mac-Naughton, another obscure pro who would one year later become a household name as one of the premier athletes and most dominant cyclists in the sport. On our final hard training ride before heading to Europe, we raced up our beloved Piuma Road in the coastal mountains of Los Angeles and recorded new PRs on the 20-plus-minute climb to the summit.

Another training partner on the ride was Tony Adler, a veteran pro who often battled the top dogs for a top-five finish in national-caliber events. Although his career was tapering off as ours began, Tony was our ultimate authority on the pro circuit. When he arrived at the summit of Piuma, trailing significantly, he breathlessly uttered the most confidence-boosting phrase I'd heard to that point in my career. With his South African lilt he proclaimed, "Wow, you guys are ready for Nice."

A couple of weeks later on the French Riviera, I discovered that Tony was right as I swam and biked with some main contenders. Off the bike, my legs felt unbelievable, and I set out at an aggressive pace on the run. I passed a dozen guys easily and found myself running with top American professional Ken Glah by mile 8. The pace felt too easy so I aggressively surged on Glah and dropped him.

Dropping one of the top long-course guys in the world as a rookie with no experience did not prove to be a wise pacing decision! Just before the turnaround, holding top-10 in the World Championships, I bonked hard and nearly blacked out. Downshifting quickly from six-minute miles to a staggering walk, I drifted over to the food table, inhaled everything I could, and walked the rest of the way home in 126th place. The experience was a good lesson in pacing and humility but confirmed that I was reaching world-class form.

Afterward, I took a three-week vacation, traveling around Europe by train on a very tight budget. I wanted to squeeze in as many cities as possible, so my strategy was to ride the train through the night, wake up in a new city, and then run all over town to enjoy the key tourist spots. I was running 8 to 12 miles a day and sometimes up to 22. Each run was an inspiring adventure in a foreign land. My budget constraints had me subsisting on bakery bread, fruit, and chocolate once destined for gifts, causing what little body fat I had to slip off. While Nice was supposed to be the end of the season, I returned home from vacation lean and fit and itching to redeem myself. I jumped right off the plane onto my bicycle and stayed there for the next two weeks, riding over 700 miles. It was time to race!

A new race series on the circuit offered up a great opportunity to compete through the winter—the Desert Princess World Championship Run-Bike-Run Series in Palm Springs, California. Organizers selected distances of 10K-62K-10K and invited an elite field of the world's best triathletes and duathletes to contest this new event in a three-race-series format, with the largest purse ever offered for duathlon racing. These distances were considered a fair compromise for the talents of the triathletes against the duathletes.

Chief among the matchups and most exciting to multisport fans was the meeting of the world's number one ranked triathlete, Scott "The Terminator" Molina, and the world's number one ranked duathlete, the undefeated Kenny Souza. These two athletes, longtime training partners, had never faced each other in competition. An excellent field of top-ranked athletes from both racing circuits filled in the field for the race. I was excited just to be a participant and took great interest in who would win the Molina-Souza duel. I had never challenged these athletes in a race and had only vague hopes of cracking the top 10. To me, the race was an opportunity to go as fast as I possibly could and enjoy the new, interesting race format.

I made an important strategy decision for such a difficult event: run very comfortably for the first 10K. I figured the race was bound to last nearly three hours and no one had completed a duathlon of this difficulty before. When the gun went off, it was obvious the rest of the field were thinking otherwise. Feeding off of the nervous energy of the pack, the entire field took off at an insane pace and soon disappeared from sight. I completed the first leg in 24th place out of 27 professionals, nearly four minutes behind the leaders! To lose this amount of time in the first event was ridiculous and pretty much eliminated any chance of a top-10 finish.

After pacing the first 10K sensibly (unlike most of the field), I flew through the bike—passing the 23 guys ahead of me—and began the second run in the lead. I was so focused on my own effort I had no idea I was leading; only when the press truck started tracking me did I bother to ask them what place I was in. I still had plenty of energy to run hard on the final 10K and build up a two-minute lead by the finish.

To me the result seemed like a miracle. With my haphazard, unstructured, fun-and-games on the European trains approach, I had just defeated two of the greatest endurance athletes in the world.

If I were to dissect the miracle, we would discover some contributing factors like hard work, a seemingly haphazard but actually scientifically sound and highly effective training schedule, an ideal mental state of no pressure or expectation, and a completely pure motivation. Focusing on running in Europe and cycling back home allowed me to achieve fitness breakthroughs in the individual sports—a common technique used by multisport athletes. My ability to vary my workouts according to energy level prevented overtraining and gave me the freedom to push my body very hard when inspired and motivated. My relaxed and pure approach allowed me to focus on my own best performance instead of blow out the first 10K with the rest of the overhyped pros.

As soon as I crossed the finish line my life changed. The media surrounded me, all of them asking the compelling question, "Who are you?"

A shocking upset victory at the Desert Princess World Championship Run-Bike-Run Series by an unknown rookie pro with no shirt. The giant Oakley glasses confirm the date circa November 1986.

CREDIT: LOIS SCHWARTZ

I floated along through the next few weeks of my life, still in a dreamlike state. I'd return home from a training session with 11 phone messages from sponsors, media, and other people who wanted my attention. At first it still felt like fun and games, but soon I felt the excitement getting to me and my life becoming more stressful.

Understand that the true definition of "stress" is any form of stimulation to the body. Stress is good because without stress we would be dead—or at least we'd never do things like learn to read, walk, speak English, develop six-pack abs, earn a degree or a paycheck, ride a bike, finish a triathlon, or learn how to use computer software. When you place the body or mind under stress, you respond by adapting and improving your skill in that area.

When we use the terms "stressed" or "stressful" we typically mean *overstress*—circumstances or events that throw us out of our normal healthy, balanced, routine comfort zone. It follows that stress does not necessarily have to be negative. You can become overstressed by positive stimulation as well. In fact, numerous stress-assessment tests cite getting married as one of the most stressful events in life, right up there with death in the family and other traumatic, negative events.

In a similar vein, my newfound success was becoming stressful. There is a difference between coming home from a hard 85-mile bike ride, eating, and taking a nap and coming home from a hard 85-mile bike ride and dealing with 11 phone messages.

I remember eagerly awaiting the publication of the feature story in *Competitor* magazine after the event. As soon as I pulled it out of my mailbox I sat down on my driveway and poured over the feature story and big photos of the shocking upset in Palm Springs. It took a few moments to register that the title, King of the Desert, referred to me! Molina gave a nice interview about how I was a talented young athlete and had a great race, then finished with a comment that was highlighted in big type: "If he wins again, he'll be puking at the finish line." I stood frozen in my driveway just staring at that quote. The Terminator, my hero, the winningest triathlete of all time, was after ME!

I consider that moment on my driveway a turning point—when I was sucked away from the innocence and pure motivation that brought me victory and thrust back into the real world. Soon I grew a grand piano on my back in the form of pressure, tension, and anxiety relating to the upcoming rematch. Since no one was more surprised than I was at my victory, I was having difficulty remaining confident and dealing with all the new attention heaped on me. I was also getting reports of Kenny Souza performing unreal workouts (like four 100-mile-plus bike rides in a single week) in San Diego, preparing for the rematch.

Instead of enjoying my workouts, I began to measure and judge them. My happiness and peace of mind were dictated by the measured result of my workouts. Sore muscles, a tickle in my throat, fatigue in the morning, or a training partner dropping me on a climb became crises that threatened my happiness and general well-being and put me in danger of humiliating myself at the next race.

Johnny G and the Calli Tea

Luckily, I had a chance meeting with someone who helped me to very quickly break out of my slump and recapture my pure power as an athlete. His name was Johnny G, and he is now a world-famous fitness celebrity and creator of the Spinning indoor cycling program. Back then Johnny was a professional ultramarathon cyclist training for the Race Across America, a grueling, nonstop 3,000-mile bike race from California to the East Coast.

We bumped into each other on the road one day outside of Los Angeles and rode together for five hours, becoming fast friends. Johnny was an intriguing, larger-than-life presence. As a personal trainer to Hollywood stars, he bubbled with the exuberance and positive energy that are prerequisites in the personal trainer game. He talked nonstop for five hours, a wild and wacky monologue of often

The one-of-a-kind Johnny G pedals across Kansas "or maybe
Oklahoma" during the 1987 Race Across America (RAAM), a
3,000-mile nonstop bicycle race from coast to coast.

CREDIT: VICTOR LAUDARE

preposterous but always positive and enthusiastic commentary on
training, competition, diet, holistic lifestyle, and more. Edgewise,
I offered Johnny a little bit of where I was at in my life and the pressure I was feeling relating to the upcoming race.

At the end of the ride, when it came time to part ways, Johnny said, "Bradley my boy, good luck. Take the burn to those guys; make them [their muscles] burn." I responded, "Ah man, I just hope I can finish in the same area code as those guys." These blatant self-deprecating comments are an epidemic among triathletes. We use self-deprecating statements and self-limiting beliefs to diffuse the pressure of being in the rat race, where your every move is measured and judged. My comment was evidence that I was not quite ready to accept my place in the sport as a legitimate competitor and challenger to the world's best. Subconsciously, I didn't feel deserving of my success.

Luckily, my comment didn't go unchecked with Johnny. As we came to a stop on the bikes, Johnny looked me in the eye and calmly said, "Bradley my boy, we must do some work together, because I can help make you a great champion. Meet me at my private gym in Beverly Hills on Tuesday at 6:30 P.M." Needless to say I was intrigued, so a few days later I drove across town on a rainy December evening into the fairy-tale land of Beverly Hills. Johnny had a beautiful, cozy private gym glistening with the latest fitness machines and plush white carpet. When I arrived, the gym was empty, the lights were out, and lit candles were everywhere. Johnny was sitting, cross-legged meditation style, in the middle of the floor. New age instrumental music drifted through the speakers.

Without speaking, Johnny motioned for me to sit across from him. Then he gestured for me to take some long, deep breaths in unison with him. For a 21-year-old punk from the Valley, the scene was quite dramatic. After about 60 seconds of deep breathing, I became mesmerized and totally focused on the moment. I could feel my entire body relax and discard the pressure and tension I had carried with me 24/7 for several weeks. Johnny proceeded to take me through a visualization session relating to the upcoming race. Through a series of questions, he had me explain in great detail everything about race day—my routine in the morning, the details of the route, my competitive strategy, and more.

He asked me to describe my competition. I lit up with excitement and started reciting the résumés of the great athletes. "Well, there's Scott Molina, the Terminator, the world's number one triathlete. He dominates at all distances and works harder than anyone. Then you have Kenny "Kaboom" Souza, previously undefeated in duathlon and national class in both running and cycling. He's been climbing Mt. Palomar in San Diego four times a week in preparation for the rematch. . . ." I rambled on, neglecting to mention myself as one of the leading contenders. Suddenly, Johnny grabbed me by the shoulders and stopped me. He looked right into my eyes and said, "Bradley, listen to me. Those guys are NOT better than you. You can beat them, but you have to believe in yourself."

It was pretty clear to Johnny that I was feeling insecure and fearful about my present situation. Over the years, I've often accused him of being psychic; he has the knack of verbalizing what I am thinking inside, even when I can't express it in words or am in denial. The timing and delivery of his message were exactly what I needed to pull out of my spiral and reawaken the pure motivation that was my greatest asset. I drifted out of the gym and floated into the night in a state of half-bliss, half-shock over what had transpired in the room.

Two days later, bursting with energy and curiosity, I decided to do something outrageous. I wanted to explode out of my trap of magazine articles, phone messages, and self-induced mental anguish. On New Year's Eve 1986, 11 days before the big showdown in Palm Springs, I took off on my bike from my home in the San Fernando Valley of Los Angeles and headed for the desolate Mojave Desert. My mission was to ride as fast as I could, as far as I could, until I became exhausted.

I warmed up and soon established a brisk pace, pedaling across the valley floor and into the mountains that rim the L.A. basin. After a few hours, I reached the Mojave Desert—long, flat, boring stretches of deserted roads where I pedaled as fast as I could for hours on end. Instead of getting tired, I felt stronger and stronger throughout the ride. After stopping for water and a snack, I snapped out of my zone for a moment and realized that I was in the middle of the Mojave Desert, 110 miles away from home, and it was going to get dark in one hour. The nearest town was Barstow, 30 miles farther into the desert.

Since I was not yet tired and I wanted to beat the darkness, I resolved to pedal all-out, at full racing speed, all the way to Barstow. I reached the finish line, Fosters Freeze in Barstow, in one hour (with a slight tailwind in the desert that day . . . campers and trailers not advised). Instead of feeling fatigued, my body was shaking from excitement as I realized I had just done something very special and was as strong in the head as I was in the legs.

As I dismounted my bike, a feeling of calmness came over me, a feeling that everything would be all right on race day. Whether I won or lost the upcoming race, I had recaptured the magic of a pure motivation. I had also smashed the artificial barriers that my mind had erected to protect me from the shock I experienced after the first victory. The reason I freaked out at the magazine article and started to measure and judge my workouts was because I didn't truly believe that I was deserving or capable of beating the world's best.

After the ride, I realized that I was deserving of the awesome feeling you get when you push your body to peak performance. Whether I was deserving of victory or deserving of getting my butt kicked would be determined on the racecourse. It was nothing to obsess over or worry about beforehand. I realized I was capable of taking on anyone in the world and that I had nothing to lose in doing so. Even though this was a solo training ride through the desert, I felt like I had just achieved a victory far more profound and impactful than winning any race. From that point on, I remained in a calm and relaxed state all the way up to the starting line on race morning. From there I floated through an absolutely effortless race and destroyed the field by five minutes.

One of the things Johnny G had me visualize was my finishing time. "Bradley, you are running strongly to the finish line and you look up at the clock. The clock says, 2 hours, 38 minutes, 45 seconds." Well, this was obviously a time Johnny had pulled out of a hat, akin to his statement on that first ride, "When I drink Calli tea with chlorella powder I get a second wind after 4 hours, 15 minutes." The experts predicted that a perfect race by a top pro on that course would result in a time of 2 hours, 45 minutes. This was in fact the time I posted to beat the top field in the first race. Two hours, 38 minutes was out of the question, but I went along with the game and half-heartedly visualized my time for Johnny.

As I came to the line in the second race, I wasn't wearing a watch and was too concerned with perfecting my celebratory gestures to notice the clock. Later I discovered that my official time was 2:38.46. You may read this and think, "coincidence," but I believe there was something far more powerful than a coincidence at play here. Johnny G planted the suggestion in my mind that I was capable of extraordinary performance if I believed in myself. Once someone plants a suggestion in your mind, it stays there until you can prove or disprove it with a belief or action.

If you tell someone, "you look fat in that dress," "you look cool in those sunglasses," "you would make a great lawyer," or "you have a nice swim stroke," you have planted a powerful suggestion that the person will then have to assess and agree with or dismiss. Those strong of mind and self-esteem will have little difficulty processing the messages of the outside world; they will either use them to their advantage ("Dude, I think she likes you—you should ask her out") or dismiss them with no harm done to their psyche. Others will allow even an offhanded comment to penetrate to the bone, creating unsettled emotions and diminished self-esteem.

This is true in success and failure. Many high achievers generate results using flawed motivations. Those who were rejected by peers or parents as a kid may spend the rest of their lives trying to prove their worth with an endless accumulation of accomplishments. Instead of being deflated by criticism or a difficult past, they use it as motivation to succeed. This impure motivation works, but it doesn't lead to happiness. There are many ways to get to the finish line—I am suggesting that a pure motivation will bring the most overall satisfaction.

Furthermore, I think that when push comes to shove, the athlete who is motivated by love and passion for the sport will be able to dig deeper and prevail over someone who is driven by superficial motivators. It's scary to let that chip slide off your shoulder; many athletes I coach bristle when I tell them to turn down the competitive volume. They envision becoming fat, lazy slobs over a 72-hour rest period.

When Johnny planted the suggestion in my mind, I was so confused that I didn't know what to make of it. I had taken down the best in the world but resisted feeling content and congruent about being a real player, let alone a favorite. I believe that is why I got the urge to pedal my brains out all day across the desert—to convince myself that I had the ability to race with the best. By the time I got to Barstow the suggestion was confirmed. I believed in myself and decided to race with a pure motivation for peak performance.

Don't Let Nobody Steal Your Joy

I never obsessed about or even verbalized a time goal of 2:38, as that could have been self-limiting. Be careful about attaching too much importance to time goals and results. When you attach your performance to a time or placing, you run the risk of limiting your potential and enjoyment. If you achieved your goal, maybe you could have gone faster but subconsciously limited yourself because you nailed your goal. If you miss your time goal, you risk artificial and illogical disappointment.

You run a similar risk if you are attached to external recognition. I remember one of my best races in high school track—a huge upset victory where I passed six guys on the final lap to win a two-mile race for a new personal record. After the race I went into the stands where my friends high-fived me and celebrated my victory. When I saw my girlfriend, she said, "Hey, how did you do?" She was in the bathroom talking to a friend during the latter stages of the race! As you may imagine, it kind of burst my bubble. Nevertheless, it was a valuable opportunity to learn the lesson of forgiveness . . . I mean the lesson of not attaching any of your happiness and satisfaction to the eyes of others!

As comedian Martin Lawrence said to his love interest in the movie *A Thin Line Between Love and Hate*: "Don't let nobody steal your joy." If you are attached to external judgments like time, place, or validation from others, you are vulnerable to getting psyched out by opponents, getting discouraged when times or places don't match expectation, and letting your anxiety limit your ultimate potential.

Let me be clear here that it is absolutely okay to set time or place goals or want to impress others and get recognition. It is okay to work toward tangible goals with great focus and dedication; you just shouldn't attach your happiness to them. You must always race with a higher and purer purpose than a superficial goal. When I coached my son's soccer team of four- and five-year-olds, I was amazed to discover that they were already clued into the emphasis our culture places on winning and counting goals. I repeated our team mantra frequently: it's okay to try as hard as you can to win, but the most important thing is to have fun.

Kids can grasp this much easier than adults can. After a particularly tough blowout loss for the soccer team, in the midst of a season where they went one and nine, I gathered the visibly disappointed kids into a circle after the game. My heart ached at the sight of 11 kids who played their hearts out and now had the look of defeat on their faces. As I launched into an encouraging, inspirational speech, I was drowned out by a call of "dog pile the coach!" Immediately they shifted from a weary, downtrodden group into a frenzied mob.

Australian Greg Welch embodied this spirit during his career perhaps better than any other professional triathlete. One dramatic example of his pure motivation and outstanding attitude came at the Hawaii Ironman races of 1993 and 1994. Welch was a race favorite during an awesome season where no one in the sport could keep pace with him on the run. On his final bike ride before flying to the island, he was struck by a car two miles from his home in San Diego and suffered a knee injury. He showed up on the island on crutches, forced to watch someone else realize the dream for which he had worked so hard.

Some were surprised to see Welchy having a jolly time in Kona, hanging out with friends, enjoying a Hawaiian vacation, and cheering for his wife Sian, a top female pro. When Welch was asked for his feelings about the accident, he said, "No use crying over spilled milk." He was able to enjoy the experience of a week at Ironman even from the sidelines. Six months later at the early season 1994 St. Croix triathlon, the disappointment of his eighth-place performance was compounded by his knee acting up again, inviting the prospect of surgery. These events would certainly be just cause to be a little bummed out.

Yet, at a party the evening of the race, Welchy seemed unaffected by his tenuous future. One of the entertainment options at this beautiful estate was a trampoline, dug into the ground right on the edge of a cliff, with a beautiful view overlooking the Caribbean. Greg couldn't resist and climbed on for a few bounces—not exactly a prudent choice for a world-class professional athlete with an injured knee.

Right then, seeing him joyfully bounce around like a little kid, I knew that whatever happened to him, he would be fine. One month later, he won a new Mazda at the Orange County triathlon, and later in the season he achieved a glorious victory at the 1994 Hawaii Ironman. Celebrating late into the evening of his Ironman victory, he

Australian Greg Welch is one of the greatest triathletes ever and the embodiment of the carefree "no worries, mate" Aussie lifestyle.

CREDIT: ELIZABETH KREUTZ

wrapped himself up like a burrito in the finish banner and started hopping around. He tripped and broke his collarbone. While your genetic makeup may hinder you from embodying the carefree "no worries, mate" Aussie lifestyle, we can all learn a profound lesson from Greg Welch's approach to the sport. If a certifiable joker can become the Hawaii Ironman champion of the world, we can all loosen up a little bit in our approach to life and triathlon.

Finishing the Palm Springs course in 2:38 was a natural by-product of the things I experienced before it. I didn't have to force or manipulate anything; it was meant to be. If Souza was meant to be the winner that day (he toasted me in the third and final race of the series, the beginning of a 44-race win streak, the longest in multisport history), the experience would have been just as powerful. Well okay, maybe not quite as powerful.

Wherever you are in the pack, when you are able to believe in yourself and stay pure and natural in your approach to the sport, that is your greatest victory. Let's look at the difference between being driven to greatness by a pure motivation and being imprisoned by the compulsive mind and the imaginary ceiling it places on your potential. If I were attached to outcomes during that first Desert Princess duathlon, I would have been demoralized upon coming in 24th out of 27 athletes in the first run. Hopelessly behind, I would have likely given up or even dropped out. On my ride to Barstow 10 days before the big rematch, I would have judged 110 miles to be a plenty long ride and my mind would have told me I was tired and ready to finish at the 110-mile mark. In reality, the first 110 miles of my ride to Barstow were just a warm-up for the physical and mental breakthroughs that happened in the next 30.

With a pure motivation that day, my mind remained focused on the present and the enjoyment of riding my bicycle as hard as I could across the desert. In the process, I was able to shatter self-limiting beliefs.

Please don't misunderstand this message as a macho chest thump. The moral of the story is not how incredible I was to hammer 140 miles and then beat everyone 10 days later in the big race. It's not about the legs; it's about the head. Step out of the rat race, feel free, take risks, push yourself to new heights, and have fun.

The World's Toughest Lesson

I had to learn this moral the hard way at another event, the 1987 World's Toughest Triathlon in Lake Tahoe, California. This popular ultradistance event boasted a brutal course and high altitude to support its presumptuous title. The event began with a 2-mile swim in 60-degree Lake Tahoe, was followed by a 100-mile bike ride over three major mountain passes, and culminated in a rugged 18-mile trail run. The race coincided with my training camp in Lake Tahoe, so I decided to jump in for workout purposes and complete just the swim and bike segments. The day before the event, I missed a car rendezvous on a training ride and ended up riding 80 miles, including a 20-mile climb from Carson City back to the lake. Needless to say, I had no expectations in the event.

With a relaxed, carefree approach, I floated through the first two events and amassed a 15-minute lead at the bike-to-run transition. One thing any pro triathlete with half a brain knows is to never drop out with a 15-minute lead! I tackled the challenging trail run and eight and a half hours later crossed the finish line the winner.

I was awakened from a nap several hours after the race by a phone call from the race director informing me that I had been disqualified. Certain that it was a prank from a friend, I was like, "Dude, who is this? Beker? What's up?" In fact it was no prank—I had been reported running a stop sign on some remote area of the bike course, in violation of the rules where the bike course was open to traffic. My initial feelings were shock and outrage. I protested the call during a lengthy meeting with race officials to no avail.

I took my frustration out on the roads, training like a madman immediately after the event. I scheduled a bunch of races in hopes of redeeming myself and my wallet. Soon, of course, I was completely exhausted, missing more races and bombing out of the Hawaii Ironman six weeks later. As time passed, I was able to reflect on the whole experience, gain a new perspective, and appreciate something deeper than whether I cashed my first-place check or not. Regardless of the DQ, I still turned in an awesome eight-and-a-half-hour performance, my first at ultradistance. I still enjoyed a wonderful day with family and friends, celebrating the beauty of Lake Tahoe and the Sierra by doing something that I loved—swimming, biking, and running. At the end of the day, I was elated with my performance and high on the endorphins and the sense of satisfaction that comes after an ultradistance effort.

Should all that change from a phone call? Of course not, but in reality many driven competitors attach much of their happiness and satisfaction to the results. I remember an incident after another race on the pro circuit, where I finished a disappointing 11th and was pedaling back to the hotel with the race winner. This athlete, $5,000 richer after a great performance, launched into a diatribe about how poorly he was treated by the race organizers, how screwy the course was, the lame awards ceremony, and the crappy hotel. The diatribe was summed up by the comment, "I hate this city. Get me out of here."

The truth is that it can happen to anyone, even a winner. We have a choice when it comes to our enjoyment of the sport. We can choose a positive attitude and a pure motivation or we can fall in line with the pack and let our happiness be dictated by results or be unhappy regardless of the result. While the choice is obvious, the important thing to focus on is that you indeed have a choice.

Lance Armstrong told me that when he was diagnosed with cancer, he gave himself "no choice but to remain positive." Here was a young world champion athlete in the prime of his life and his career whose world was turned upside down after one visit to the doctor's office. Even with the sudden delivery of a grave diagnosis, Lance chose a positive attitude. It is hard to imagine a more dramatic example of how attitude can help you overcome difficult circumstances. When you cultivate a pure motivation, you are able to break free from the stress, anxiety, and frequent setbacks that come with a compulsive approach and learn powerful lessons about becoming a happier, healthier, and more balanced person. Pure motivation enables your mind and body to become truly connected—you govern your training decisions by the messages that your body and emotions send your brain. This enables you to proceed without interruption on the path to peak performance and avoid the illness, injuries, and burnout of the mind-body disconnect.

CHAPTER 2

HOW TO ESCAPE
THE RAT RACE

"The problem with the rat race is that even if you win,
you're still a rat."

—LILY TOMLIN

Even If You Win, You're Still a Rat

It's a challenge to cultivate a natural and balanced approach in the modern world. We are subjected to the overwhelming daily pressures of the rat race—to respond to advertising and consume to the point of decadence, to accumulate stuff and live in fear of losing it, and to judge yourself and others on a superficial, material level. It's more common to hear something like, "Meet my friend Steve, he's a VP over at Merrill and did a 10:38 at Hawaii last year," as opposed to, "Meet my friend Steve, he spends a lot of quality time with his daughter, values his health over material achievement, and helps out his elderly neighbor." It feels normal and comfortable to be a member of the rat race.

When you plow through life, you usually get ahead by conventional definition. There is nothing wrong with that; the influences of our genetics and life experience make many of us highly productive, energetic beings who constantly seek new challenges. Going against your basic nature to sit on the beach all day feels unnatural. If I'm going on vacation to Hawaii, I'd rather hike in the mountains, play golf, snorkel, surf, eat healthy, and relax on the beach a little bit than vegetate on the beach all day and eat and drink to excess. Balance is the answer to everything, and if you discover that your balance point is closer to the active end than the inactive end, that's great.

However, it's important to recognize how easy it is to cross over the balance line with physical training and how detrimental this crossover can be to your performance and enjoyment of the sport. If you work too hard at your job, you are likely to get promoted, recognized, and rewarded for your hard efforts. If you work too much at your physical training, you are likely to get crushed in competition and sick, injured, or burned out. Sometimes getting ahead is bad—especially when you get ahead of yourself.

Andrew MacNaughton once said, "The great thing about racing a long-distance triathlon is that you get to experience a lifetime of emotions in a single day." The racecourse offers completely straightforward, honest, graphic, and intense lessons about success and failure. If you feel strong, perform well, and have a great time, you are successful. If you get your butt kicked or don't enjoy the experience, you have failed.

In real life it's possible to distract yourself from these important lessons. You can connive and schmooze to get ahead in business, and all the world sees is your new Escalade—not the people you put off, the deceptive advertising campaign you ran, or the moral standards you bent along the way. Or you can have a wonderful career, be well liked, respected, and compensated, but remain deficient in other areas of your life. Perhaps you become distant from your family and friends or physically unhealthy from your devotion to work.

These lessons are not easy to recognize because they are nuances blended into a fast-paced life. Constant stimulation and distraction are defining features of the rat race. When you're at the park in the sandbox with your kids and you climb out to talk on your cell phone, it may take you five years to appreciate the significance of your mistake. One day it hits you: your kids aren't in the sandbox anymore and they never will be again.

When you get on the racecourse it's different; everything is clearer. If you overtrain, undertrain, or neglect an event like swimming because you don't like it or fear it, these elements of imbalance or inattention will show up in the wash. Even if you succeed, you may be left with an empty feeling (the "post-ironman blues" are common enough to be written about and studied extensively) if your approach was unnatural or imbalanced. Think about the athlete who is standing on the podium receiving his Olympic gold medal but who has taken performance-enhancing drugs in pursuit of victory. I can't imagine what's going on in his head (some heavy rationalization perhaps?), but it can't be as satisfying as it is for someone with a natural, healthy, and balanced approach.

Stolen Wallets and Leaky Sunroofs

When Tim DeBoom went to the 2003 Hawaii Ironman as two-time defending champion, he suffered the extremely painful misfortune of passing a kidney stone out on the run course and a dramatic DNF.

His postrace comments indicated that he had learned a profound and valuable lesson from the ordeal: "I don't know what was more painful—what I experienced physically or what I experienced emotionally. The Ironman is definitely a metaphor for life. This sport has brought me the greatest successes and the greatest disappointments of my adult life. You can't have one without the other. I think we all learn that at some point."

32

Two-time Hawaii Ironman champ Tim DeBoom of Lyons, Colorado, displays the champion's quality of learning and improving from both success and failure . . . and having ripped legs.

CREDIT: ELIZABETH KREUTZ

One memorable learning experience in my life was getting my wallet stolen at the movies. I had just returned from a triathlon in Mexico, where I was recognized for my performance and reimbursed for travel expenses with an envelope filled with a substantial amount of cash. I had been meaning to go to the bank, but I was still heavy when I went to the movies.

Well, we were unfortunate enough to sit right in front of a few talkative young ladies, so in the middle of the movie, after a series of unsuccessful "shushes," we decided to move to other seats across the theater. My wallet remained, stuffed in the drink cup at my old seat. (I had no pockets in my sweatpants—does this still count as getting my wallet "stolen"?) In any case, I had traveled far, swum in a filthy, oil-slicked ocean, climbed massive hills, threaded through a traffic jam on a dangerously congested bike course, and run my butt off in tropical heat for that money. This particular day was certainly the most money I had ever had in my wallet, and I chose that day to lose the wallet.

Once the wallet was gone, I had a choice of how to handle the experience. I could let anger and sorrow bring me down or move on and take something positive from the experience. I decided that the positive element I could apply from the experience was not to worry excessively about money or misfortune. The rules and regulations of the rat race have created an epidemic illness aptly described by the title of the bestselling book *Affluenza*. The consumerism and fear mentality that have infected our culture often lead to flawed and stress-producing attitudes about money.

Many people have a "scarcity" mentality about money. Hoard whatever you can, compete with other people to take money from the economy in order to consume for personal needs, and build personal wealth. A scarcity mentality views the economy as a single pie with the goal to eat as big a slice as possible.

A healthier mentality could be described as one of abundance. Someone with an abundant mentality about money sees it for what it is—a mere symbol of value to exchange in the economy. Money is not a scarce natural resource like a rain forest. With an abundant mentality, you see many pies and raw ingredients. It is possible to contribute additional economic value by baking a pie. In doing so, you are able to enjoy a hefty slice for yourself and enable others who help you to enjoy slices, too.

A philosophy of abundance encourages generosity, sharing of resources, and positive attitudes about money. As confirmed by many experts and bestselling financial books, you can still become wealthy with an abundant mentality. With that attitude, you are better able to deal with setbacks like a $30 parking ticket on your window, a stock price declining from $68 to $12 in six months, or overpaying for dinner.

My friend Dr. Steve Kobrine, whose license plate reads "No Worys," has lived by that creed as well as anyone I know. He's been a competitive runner for over 20 years, earned a mathematics degree from UC Berkeley at age 20, and later became a family physician. He's definitely a high-achieving, goal-oriented person. Yet he follows this path without the worries or stress so common in the type-A personality.

Steve bought an economy car during college and decided to get a sunroof installed. He had the installation done at an aftermarket shop and soon discovered that the sunroof leaked. He took it back to the shop to get it fixed, only to discover at his next car wash that it still leaked! At this point he decided to go to the dealer to get the job done right, paying more than the original cost of the job. I asked why he didn't return a third time to the chop shop and either have them fix it satisfactorily or demand his money back. His answer, "They obviously did a lousy job. Now the sunroof works. My peace of mind is more important than going back there."

Project this mentality to see if it can help you tackle the problems that you face in your own life, especially in your athletic career. Steve took responsibility for his mistake (going to the chop shop in the first place) instead of the more basal route of blaming the chop shop and banging his head against the wall (or the sunroof) to try and force things to be right. He pursued the goal of peace of mind rather than fight to change the reality that he went to a crappy sunroof shop.

Sometimes we must take a step back from the rat race to remember that we can't control what happens. We can only control our own attitudes and actions. This is a challenge for the compulsive athlete who has a natural desire to control environment and results. When you feel stressed that the world does not unfold exactly as you want it to, you need to take a step backward and adopt a different attitude.

At the 1992 International Triathlon Union (ITU) World Championships in Muskoka, Canada, we woke up to a very thick fog that completely obscured our beautiful lake venue. Soon an announcement came that the race would be delayed until the first buoy was visible from shore. For many athletes in a pressure-packed situation like world championships race morning, the fog delay was an incredible source of stress. Those perfect (compulsive) prerace routines of consuming an energy bar and a bottle of one and a half scoops of Cytomax exactly two hours before the race, jogging for fifteen minutes, stretching for seven, and then dressing for the race were thrown out of whack. We didn't even have information about how long the delay would last.

I could see the stress level building among the athletes around me and resolved to do something different. While everyone milled around the race start watching the fog and bugging the officials for more news, I went back to sleep in my room, requesting that our team manager wake me when the officials finally announced the start time. The start ended up being delayed until early afternoon! I performed to my abilities that day and enjoyed a fifth-place finish. Many athletes were thrown off their peak performance by the delay as confirmed by all the complaining at the awards ceremony that evening.

When you care deeply about superficial results, about your ego demands, and about what others think of you, you are ensconced in the rat race lifestyle. As the years go by and you travel more miles down this road, it becomes more and more difficult to pull out of it. A change of mind-set and behavior might seem as difficult as giving away all of your worldly possessions and joining an ashram.

There is so much support for this high-stress lifestyle that it takes tremendous momentum to break free and choose a different path. Athletics can be that powerful vehicle to facilitate true lifestyle change, because the results of your actions are so graphic and dramatic. I'll never forget how I resolved to go with the flow of the fog on the lake and how deeply relaxing that nap was during the morning hours of world championships day.

Vegas, Baby!

It often takes outrageous behavior to break ingrained patterns and habits. When you stretch yourself by doing something different, uncomfortable, and unnatural, the experience will have a bigger impact. Pro triathlete couple Greg Bennett and Laura Reback—both among the world's best—say they try to socialize with people who have never heard of a triathlon. They are aware of the need to balance their lives as they engage in an all-consuming sport.

In this section, I will discuss my Purposeful Anticompulsive Strategy, which involves doing something creative, uncomfortable, and outrageous to break through negative, compulsive patterns and experience personal growth. I will ask you to choose a habit, behavior pattern, or obsession that has control over you or limits your enjoyment and peak performance in life. The moment you become purposeful toward a bad habit, you reclaim control over your habits and your lifestyle.

Those who are stressed about time will feel like they are constantly squeezed, like there is never enough time in the day to do all that they want. Doing nothing for five minutes or doing a relaxed breathing and stretching ritual for five minutes to start your day is a way to take control over time and realize that you will always have a choice of how to spend your time. In addition, a few minutes of breathing exercises can stimulate alpha brain wave activity (detailed in the book *The Relaxation Response* by Dr. Herbert Benson). The alpha brain state is characterized by very slow brain waves and is the most restorative time for your brain. When you can calm your mind and relax your body on demand by properly conducting a simple breathing awareness exercise, you will enjoy a dramatic improvement in your time management and recover from various forms of stress in your life.

My suggestion is to engage in some purposeful anticompulsive behavior, both in your athletics and in your real life, in an effort to stimulate thought and behavior change. Here are some examples of anticompulsive behavior that may be relevant to your lifestyle and generate growth experiences:

- Do nothing for five minutes a day. Sit outside and watch the clouds, or listen to the sounds in your environment.
- Take off your watch and run as far as you can until you can't continue. Call and get a lift home.
- Go to Las Vegas for a day on short notice—gamble, drink, eat decadent foods, stay out late, act crazy, blow money on high-risk casino bets.
- If you keep an obsessively detailed training log, do not record workouts for two weeks.
- Complete an awesome workout and don't tell anyone about it (from Mark Allen's *Total Triathlete* book).
- Do not time any workout for two weeks.
- Ride your bike from sunrise to sunset.
- Perform an outrageous act of kindness for a stranger.
- Purposely leave the last few bites of food on your plate, even if you are still hungry.
- Leave a huge tip to someone performing a minor service.

- If you are in a big hurry, let people cut in front of you in line or take a longer route to your destination.
- During a drive home, pull over and get out of your car. Sit and do nothing for five minutes.
- Give someone else credit for something you thought of or did.
- Buy two of something even though you need only one.
- Leave the race site before getting your results.

Even when you are in a traffic jam with no control over how long your trip will take, you can still choose to relax and adopt a positive attitude. You can let go of your anxiety about time whenever you want. In doing so, you are able to manipulate time to your own benefit. As Einstein proved, time is relative to the observer. When you are having fun, time flies and an hour goes by quickly. When you are bored or doing something you don't like, time can drag to the extent that those same 60 minutes seem like an eternity.

While we all know that 60 minutes is 60 minutes and can be quantified by a watch or clock, the only relevance an hour has is how we perceive it. Meditation is supposed to help you experience these truths; quiet the mind and you can make time stand still. To all but the most skilled practitioners, this seems like mumbo jumbo.

I have struggled through many failed attempts to quiet the mind and meditate. Every time I assume the lotus position, my knees start to ache or I remember that I have to call someone or add an item to the grocery list. However, I have experienced the phenomenon of time standing still a few times while training and racing. One of the most profound occasions came on a bike ride from my home in Auburn to South Lake Tahoe—a monster 140-mile journey over the Sierra with 14,000 feet of climbing. About three hours into the ride, I began an ascent on a quiet, secondary mountain road called Mormon Emigrant Trail. A few minutes later, I noticed that I had reached the summit of Carson Pass—8,500 feet at the top of the Sierra range.

In reality, the climb lasted about 35 miles and ascended 4,000 feet—nearly four hours of riding time. During that time, I drifted into such a rhythm that I released my obsession with time and experienced a complete absorption into the present activity of pedaling my bicycle up the road. The climb truly felt like it lasted only a few minutes. When I noticed the Carson Pass summit sign, it was as if an alarm clock had gone off in my mind and I had woken up to reality again after a four-hour detour to bicycle fairy-tale land. The sensation is difficult to convey in words, but it convinced me that time is relative and that you can use the power of this truth to your advantage.

With apologies to the spiritual adepts ensconced in hillside monasteries doing seven-day silence retreats, this is meditation at its finest. All you have to do is go long; you don't even have to shave your head or part with worldly possessions.

Fear and Consumerism

While most of us entered the sport with a healthy, relaxed approach, we typically reach a turning point in response to competitive stimulus. Once you finish a few races with encouraging results, your mind begins to whirl with the "more is better" thinking that is endemic to American culture. Corporate advertising has fueled the most rabid consumerism in the history of the planet. Our brains have been programmed since childhood to believe that bigger and better equate to happiness—better job, bigger office, bigger car, bigger house, bigger bank account, bigger meal portions. Thus, it's natural to apply the same thinking and behavior to our triathlon career—or anything else we do.

Model and yoga instructor Colleen Saidman said, "As a model, you're thrown into a completely materialistic world, where the answers are 'bigger, better, and more.' But the real answers are quieter and subtler." Try replacing "model" with "triathlete" and reflecting on Colleen's quote. As a professional competing for my groceries and house payment, it was a challenge to internalize this message. It's hard to appreciate the quiet, subtle lessons when I'm getting my butt kicked. I prefer to learn the loud, dramatic lessons of victory! However, upon reflecting over my career, I realized a couple of important things:

- I learned more profound and lasting lessons in defeat than in victory.
- When my motivation was pure, I was able to perform at my peak.

Pure motivation is a catch-22 that is little understood by the athletic world and certainly not by the material world. The saying, "that which you want most becomes the hardest to obtain" is highly relevant. When my motivations drifted away from pure toward impure—when I focused on things like money, media coverage, beating other athletes—I made bad decisions. I forced my body to do workouts or improve at a rate faster than was naturally meant to be. Or I would decide where to race based on financial incentive rather than the ideal where and when of peak performance. In a sport where being 2 percent off peak means the difference between winning a large amount of money or breaking even in sixth place, an impure motivation can be devastating.

My four college roommates and I used to have long conversations about our struggle to understand and succeed in relationships with the opposite sex. We pondered the theory that if you really liked someone intensely, working the angle became more difficult and emotional stress increased. With anxiety and desperation present, one would have a tendency to make all the wrong moves (unlike Tom Cruise) and blow the deal (unlike Donald Trump). Alternatively, if you really liked someone and were able to play it cool, enjoy the

Paula Newby-Fraser and Greg Welch, two of the greatest triathletes, also have a talent for relaxing and having fun.

PHOTO: ELIZABETH KREUTZ

experience, and go with the flow, things usually ended up in the best place.

Well, it's quite a bit more difficult for the triathlete to proceed along this path than for someone in a yoga class. The sport is grueling and highly competitive, and the results are graphic and dramatic. There is tremendous momentum from peers and the outside world to define yourself by tangible results.

Unfortunately, I had varying degrees of success maintaining a pure motivation over the course of my career. After I beat the best in the world as an unknown rookie with a totally innocent and pure approach to the sport, I was sucked away from pure motivation and into the rat race. In a consuming sport like triathlon, it's easy to get caught up in being a triathlete instead of remembering who you are—someone who does triathlons.

When I was caught up with impure motivations, I would force the issue in training and generally increase stress levels in my life. After a resulting string of poor races, I became disgusted with my approach and my competitive failures and took a break. The break was not only physical (reduced training volume and skipping races) but mental, too. I chucked all the pressure out the window and, when I was sufficiently rested, returned to serious training with fresh enthusiasm and perspective. Invariably I would enjoy great competitive results.

The cycle had a tendency to repeat itself, especially when the stakes escalated as my career progressed. During the best season of my career in 1991, I was positioned to win the biggest prize in the sport—$30,000 for the Coke Grand Prix/Bud Light US Triathlon Series points winner. As the dream was fast becoming a reality, I began to feel overwhelmed by the pressure, attention, and logistics of being on top. When I went on a seven-race win streak, I started each successive race with the fear, pressure, and expectation that come when you are expected to win.

Again, it's a catch-22, because you can't expect to just float to the top on a fun cloud in any competitive arena. I was intensely competitive and extremely driven to achieve my athletic goals, or I would not have achieved them. However, one must find a balance and not become attached to results. It's okay to strive mightily for victory, but you have to walk away and forget about it after the race is over.

We see a manifestation of this fearful, more-is-better epidemic when it comes to the massive equipment and service purchases of triathletes. This is good news for people like racing bicycle manufacturers, who have seen business boom and prices of a triathlon racing bike skyrocket. A 2003 survey of *Velo News* magazine subscribers indicated that the average purchase price of a new road bike is $2,923. Certainly you need at least an average bike! You may even think that you need the best of equipment, coaching, and nutrition to succeed on the racecourse.

The need for the trappings and toys of the rat race is often matched by an emotional drive of the same nature. Emotionally, you may place great importance on external recognition and other matters of the ego. You may be driven by an obsessive need for constant validation.

There is nothing wrong with wanting to indulge in the best equipment, wear sleek training clothes to show off a tight body, and enjoy the other perks and fringe benefits that come with the triathletic lifestyle. I think it's disingenuous and transparent to pretend you are above it all. It's like those athlete interviews where the narrator says, "There's no sign that you're in the home of a legend," or the athlete says, "My gold medal is in a drawer somewhere." Yeah, right. I think it's better to be like 2000 Olympic triathlon gold medalist Simon Whitfield who proudly shares his gold medal with the school children he talks to across Canada.

The danger comes in skewing your viewpoint to place a priority on toys, your appearance, or anything else superficial. This pushes you away from a natural approach and back toward the fear and consumption-driven rat race approach. Consider that you can spend thousands of extra dollars to save a few pounds of weight on your racing bicycle, but you can also improve your dietary habits to drop a few extra pounds of fat to achieve even more performance benefit!

CHAPTER 3

THE MYTH OF SUFFERING

Free Food and Massage, Next Left

It is important to adjust your mentality and discard the belief that suffering and a stubborn will are keys to being a successful triathlete. While we may be playing with semantics here, you can make a clear distinction between "struggling" or "suffering" and "pushing" your body in the context of your training and racing. Think of the difference between these two statements that describe a tough workout:

- "I was really suffering, just hatin' life, on that hill."
- "I was really pushing it to maximum effort on that hill."

Struggling and suffering are reflexive words—implying that some outside element is inflicting pain upon you against your will. While Lance Armstrong and other champions often use words like these to describe the truth of their professions, their mind-sets are internally driven. They are in control of their efforts; they choose to compete at championship level and push their bodies to the point of "suffering." It would be more accurate to use a word describing self-initiated action like "pushing" or "striving" when describing the competitive efforts of champions.

You should not have to suffer as much as *strive* to get 100 percent effort from your body in a race. If you watch the Tour on television, it sure looks like Lance and the rest are suffering. Yes, but their stance, their mind-set, remains aggressive, as in, "bring on the pain and suffering that comes from pushing the body to maximum effort. I am ready and willing to accept it and test myself."

When Lance says that he loves to suffer on the bike, you have to look at what he really means. He loves to push himself on the bike and grow as a person through athletic challenges. Lance's only true suffering came when he was in a hospital bed dealing with the effects of cancer treatment.

When the going gets tough in a race or training session, it can be extremely beneficial to your morale to shift your mentality from suffering to striving. When endurance efforts become difficult, success is often determined by your mentality—whether positive or negative thoughts prevail. If you consider some samples of your internal dialogues during a tough race, they are typically a battle between positive and negative thoughts.

In the middle of tough races, I would often think things like, "Why am I doing this?"; "Can't I find a more reasonable career?"; "I don't care if this guy beats me—fourth is still good money." These thoughts would surface and then square off with more empowering thoughts like, "A top three here would kick in an additional grand in bonuses"; "Only two more miles, keep forcing the pace and these guys will fold"; "You've traveled all the way across the world for this; just give your best effort." When I was in contention and performing at a high level, the positive thoughts always won out. Yep, it's okay to have superficial thoughts and motivators (money, glory, impressing the girl who is watching) as long as they are positive and empowering. When I was physically off-form and battling for a spot far back in the pack, the negative thoughts won out and my performance showed it.

When I crossed the finish line of a hard-fought victory over tough competition—a peak performance—I was exhausted physically but my spirit was soaring. When I struggled in races where I was physically depleted, ill-prepared, or had a negative mentality, I finished physically exhausted and with my spirit crushed.

Sometimes the negative thoughts indicate a larger problem and prevail to teach you a lesson. It is very important to recognize the times when you are not meant to push your body to peak performance. Ideally, you would grasp this before the gun goes off or before your flight leaves and skip the race. Racing is a precious gift that must never be disrespected or squandered. You should race only when you are 100 percent physically and mentally prepared for peak performance. After all, "you only have so many races in you and then you lose your will," said Andrew MacNaughton.

In the 1993 Ironman New Zealand, I was holding seventh place on the run course with 10 miles to go. At that point, the course passed right by the finish line before proceeding on an out-and-back segment to complete the 26-mile route. By the halfway point, I could feel my iliotibial (I.T.) band stiffening, an injury I had been fighting to keep under control for the previous few years. It grew progressively worse over the next few miles, reducing me to a survival shuffle by the time I reached the finish venue at mile 16. It wasn't disastrous—I certainly could have finished—but it could have become a serious injury after 10 more miles of pavement. As I glanced quickly over to the finish area, I saw an incredible spread of untouched food and rows of empty massage tables. I took a hard left off the racecourse and went straight for the food, a massage, and an ice pack for my knee.

You may wonder why, after flying across the Pacific Ocean, racing hard for seven hours, and holding a top-10 position in a prestigious international event, I would just pull the plug. I did it because I was more concerned with the health of my knee and my higher goals of contending for victory in the shorter races that were my specialty. I didn't feel the least bit of shame or regret in pulling out of that race or any other one that was a willful decision; it all depends on your purpose for competing.

Personally, I feel that too much fuss is made over the valiant efforts to finish races at all costs. It can often be just as honorable to drop out—or not even start—when your health or well-being is compromised and accept it with grace. I enjoyed my trip to New Zealand and my seven hours on the racecourse. While I would have much preferred an ending that saw me breaking the victory tape, the ending that came was the one that was meant to be, and I had to accept it.

Pardon me for butting in on your personal code of honor and athletic value system, but perhaps you can consider the relative importance of finishing for a moment. I have heard so many athletes swell with pride when reporting their record of finishing every race or getting to the finish line despite adversity, injury, and fatigue.

Many parents think that teaching their kids to never give up is one of the basic foundations of child rearing—right up there with saying "please" and "thank you." This motto deserves a deeper examination. There are lots of important values to teach children, including giving their best effort and keeping commitments. However, it's also important to show them a world where the experience means more than the results. Then they can develop the courage to think for themselves and create the life that they want.

World champion amateur duathlete and triathlete Mary Dunn of Chesire, Connecticut, commented, "Many successful people have had the message driven into them from childhood that, 'you are not allowed to fail; never give up; suck it up; turn the other cheek, etc.' Those are destructive messages if not balanced with reality and recognizing that we don't have to give 100 percent all of the time. It's even okay to give up when we think it is a healthier decision to do so."

Whatever turns you on is great, but don't forget you are guaranteed to finish life at some point no matter what. Perhaps you can enjoy yourself along the way without manufacturing pressures and expectations to finish everything that you start. If your athletic goal can evolve from "finish no matter what" to "pursue peak performance," it can be a positive step. If your kid does not like piano lessons, is not developing a love of music from taking piano lessons, and has a negative attitude toward piano lessons, perhaps it is time to discuss the option of quitting. What I look forward to is helping teach my children the skills to distinguish when to stick it out and when it's time to quit. If something is suffering—your mind, body, or attitude—shift your mentality to striving. If you can't, go get a massage and a good meal and forget about it.

Mental Toughness Is for Wimps

Most triathletes think the key to success is to follow a consistent training schedule, have the best equipment, and develop the mystical "mental toughness" that enables them to persevere when things get difficult in workouts or races.

49

Mental toughness and confidence are things that fall into place naturally. You can't buy them or rub them on like a temporary tattoo. Therefore, they should not warrant the consideration that most triathletes pay to them. Sure, you can exercise a stubborn will out on the lava fields (or any racecourse that seems like lava fields in the latter stages!) and drag your battered body to the finish line. What's the big deal? For all but a small percentage of athletes at the back of the pack for whom merely finishing is a true peak performance, finishing a race for the sake of finishing can be more obsessive than honorable. This might be hard for many readers to agree with.

In the rat race, someone who takes on the competition and increases market share, brand awareness, and profit margin is considered a hero. Fight hard, never give up, be mentally tough, and kill your opponents. This stubborn will concept seems to be the main theme of the business world and the self-help motivational books, audiotapes, and seminars from today's leading gurus. Consequently, it also seems to be the main redeeming quality and character lesson from triathlon. This is thanks in no small part to the heavily dramatized TV programs of triathlon and other sports.

It was quite dramatic to see two-time Ironman defending champ Tim DeBoom pass a kidney stone on the run course of the marathon during the 2003 Hawaii Ironman TV program. I guess that tactless close-up shot inside the ambulance makes for good TV, but it is not relevant to his career as a champion athlete. He should be lauded and celebrated for his victories, not his struggles. The same is true for Julie Moss. Her crawl to the finish in the 1982 Ironman put the sport on the map and is burned in the memory of triathletes everywhere. However, the most powerful memory I choose to have of Julie Moss is not her sprawled out on the pavement in Kona, it's her storming to the turnaround on the run course of the 1989 World Cup Australia tri, on the way to her biggest victory and most amazing run.

While it is powerful and inspiring to see triathletes struggle against the odds and cross the finish line successfully, I don't think that struggle and suffering should be the central element of your triathlon experience or the triathlon ideal. Most of the people who are driven enough to get themselves into a predicament like running 13 or 26 miles after several hours of swimming and biking don't really need to hone their stubborn will skills.

This misuse of mental toughness may be a contributing factor to a mediocrity epidemic in our sport that I will discuss later in this chapter. Applying mental toughness and a stubborn will to workouts that are intuitively wrong will fatigue you and sabotage your fitness. Applying mental toughness and a stubborn will to struggle to the finish line can often scar you long term. Few will forget Mark Allen in the 1987 Ironman, where his four-minute lead at mile 22 of the marathon evaporated and he struggled across the finish line 10 minutes behind Dave Scott, looking dangerously exhausted and emaciated. He was suffering from internal bleeding and rushed to the hospital, where he spent several days recovering.

If your compelling purpose in life is to win the Ironman, climb Mt. Everest, or make an NFL roster, you definitely need to compromise your health on the path to these goals. Few are inclined to play these high-risk games. After all, the five people who die for every 100 who attempt Mt. Everest are a real buzz kill. If triathlon had a similar mortality rate, would you still be a competitive triathlete? Even the most serious world-class amateur competitor will hopefully agree that athletic pursuits are not worth risking or compromising long-term health.

In the early 1980s, a triathlete acquaintance of mine went to a race in Mexico, where he pushed valiantly to finish an extremely difficult course in steamy tropical conditions. He was overcome by heat stroke at the finish line and was hospitalized. While he lived to tell the story and race another day, he sustained permanent damage to his body. From then on, in races with even moderate heat and humidity, his natural cooling system would malfunction and his body would shut down. His finishing the race in Mexico was a brilliant display of mental toughness deserving of an award. But who wants to receive an award from a hospital bed?

When I asked Lance Armstrong about his mental training and preparation for competition, he revealed that he gave them *little thought*! To Lance, the important thing is to do the physical work on the road and live a life that is congruent with his purpose of winning the Tour de France. If triathletes were to take note of this message, they would likely suffer less in races and perform better. This would allow them to learn the important lessons of competitive excellence and discard the superficial ones—like how to struggle and push on with a stubborn will.

When you train and live correctly, racing becomes less of a sufferfest and more of the peak performance experience it should be. This revelation came to me at the very beginning of my endurance athletic career. At the age of 14, on a whim, I entered a local 10K road race. Armed with a handful of 20-minute training jogs, I toed the line and raced flat out for 6.2 miles. While I finished in a respectable time of 38:47, I was shattered by the effort. For most of the day, I was flat on my back suffering from an endless wave of stomach cramps and nausea. This happened after several more races, including during my first year as a high school cross-country runner.

As I learned more about running and mixed with some elite athletes, I was astonished to notice that they could race a flat-out 10K and then go for a three-mile cooldown jog within minutes of finishing! I had a similar amount of competitive drive as the elite runners, but my experience of racing involved more pain and suffering of the wrong kind. Only when I escalated my training and commitment to an athletic lifestyle (like not eating a huge breakfast an hour before races) was I able to approach the sport like an athlete.

52

Sleeping in for Peak Performance

Many triathletes struggle with when to rest and when to push themselves. Sometimes your intuitive voice of reason and restraint whispers that you should flake on a workout or drop some items on your ambitious daily agenda. Then, the obsessive type-A voice in your head typically screams, "get out the door you lazy slob!"—drowning out the voice of reason. After all, if you flaked every time you didn't feel like doing something, you would never have (fill in the blank) made it through college, got elected to city council, finished your first triathlon, been promoted through the ranks to vice president, raised three kids, etc. You would probably be a slacker living in a van down by the river.

When I was a rookie pro triathlete visiting my girlfriend and now wife Tracy in San Diego, I got up the courage to phone Scott Tinley and ask to join him on his Sunday morning 20-mile run. We agreed to meet at a certain time, and I hung up the phone excited to spend some time on the trails with a big shot in the sport. I was feeling a little overtrained at the time, but certainly the opportunity to run with Tinley outweighed the fact that I needed some rest. The next morning I slept hard through my alarm and woke up feeling totally cooked some 45 minutes after our scheduled departure time. Later that day at a wedding, I saw Tinley and apologized profusely. "Apologize for what?" he asked.

"For blowing you off on the run this morning."

"Oh, I forgot all about that. I was in bed till noon!" he said.

On another visit to San Diego, I remember participating in the world famous "Tuesday Run"—a brisk 12-mile fartlek session along the horse trails in the wealthy enclave of Rancho Santa Fe. Each week, a pack of as many as 80 people would knock heads on this run, including some of the leading athletes in multisport. I remember standing in the parking lot after a grueling workout and noticing a lone figure running in, a few minutes behind the last runners in the pack. Poor guy, I thought, a straggler behind the stragglers. As the runner got closer I recognized him as Mark Allen, the greatest triathlete in history and ranked number one in the world at that time. I hadn't seen Mark all morning and assumed he had missed the workout. I asked him what happened, and he explained that he had overslept, arrived a few minutes late to the start, and just did his own thing behind the pack.

Seeing Mark cruise in alone was an interesting contrast to the mentality of most of the Tuesday Run participants. If a workout was ever like a race, this was the one. The Tuesday Run was where you showed your cards and determined how you stacked up against your competition. The lead pack on the Tuesday Run mirrored the guys with the best run splits on the world circuit. But Mark Allen, a fixture in the front of that pack, had an intuitive sense not to mix it up with the pack on that particular morning. Furthermore, he didn't seem troubled or stressed by missing the big, intense macho battle at the front of the pack on a particular early-season Tuesday morning run. Whether his oversleeping was subconscious, deliberate, or completely innocent (I don't think he ever overslept for a prize-money race!) was not important; the insights I gained by watching him bring up the rear that day were profound.

The Mediocrity Epidemic

I believe that many triathletes suffer from a state of mild to severe fatigue year-round as a result of type-A rat race lifestyle compounded by chronic overtraining. As a consequence, we see an aggregate performance level that is, in my opinion, mediocre. This may not be a very popular opinion, and I don't wish to denigrate the wonderful and inspiring efforts delivered by triathletes everywhere, but I will suggest that average finish times could improve dramatically if athletes approached the sport in a more natural and pure manner.

A top male professional can complete an iron-distance course in favorable conditions in around eight hours, a top female in around nine hours. Excepting the performances of a select few outstanding national-caliber amateurs, most competitors are extremely far behind the standard set by the world's best. In my opinion, many amateur triathletes in the "peak performance" age groups from 25 to 40 (a span where age does not hinder peak potential performance), training an average of 10 to 20 hours a week, with low body fat and a strong background of years in endurance athletics should finish closer to the pros than they do. The same is true for the age-adjusted performances of older athletes.

For many athletes, the collective return on investment just does not seem to be there for the incredible amount of time that they spend training. The Hawaii Ironman World Championships is the most selective mass field in all of triathlon. Almost all of the field must gain entry by placing highly in a series of qualifying events throughout the

The Hawaii Ironman World Championships—a very long race in a very hot place that has become the pinnacle of the sport. Some 1,500 athletes from around the globe meet strict qualifying standards to participate. Even a top pro like Japan's Shingo Tani is spent at the finish line.

CREDITS: ELIZABETH KREUTZ

preceding year around the world. (A small percentage of the field gains entry by lottery.)

At the 2003 Hawaii Ironman World Championships, the median time among the 1,569 finishers was 11:12, nearly three hours behind the male winner, Peter Reid. A survey of the Hawaii Ironman participants in 2000 revealed an average weekly training volume of 15,000 yards swimming, 248 miles cycling, and 48 miles running!

This is a massive amount of weekly training (not far behind the average of the professional competitors) conducted by the most accomplished endurance athletes in all the age groups and from around the world.

Triathletes can argue this point at a carbo-load dinner for hours, but even when you make adjustments and allowances for age, reduced training volume, genetic potential limitations, and lifestyle considerations (for example, a real job), I still think the return on investment is missing for the amount of time spent training. I believe this is true not only for the elite field in Hawaii but among casual triathletes. At the 2003 Accenture Chicago Triathlon, which boasts the world's largest field and is open to anyone, the median time for the 400 racers in the popular 35 to 39 male age group was over an hour behind the professional race winner at an Olympic distance.

The world of marathon running seems to be similarly mediocre. In a large race like the Los Angeles Marathon, which had 16,788 finishers in 2003, a time of 3:00 was good for 105th—inside the top 1 percent of finishers. Three hours has long been considered a performance standard that designates one as a serious, accomplished marathon runner. A time of 4:00 was in the first 2,000 finishers or top 12 percent of the field. A four-hour marathon pace equates to 9:10 per mile. Run slower than nine-minute miles and your pace switches to a jog, shuffle, or walk. So 88 percent of the runners in a big marathon like L.A.'s are not running at even a moderate competitive pace.

This may not necessarily be such a bad thing. Legendary miler and popular track commentator Marty Liquori said this about the current rebirth of the running boom, which originated in the early 1970s, petered out steadily over the next couple decades, and then saw a massive explosion around the new millennium: "The first running boom, which was much smaller than the current one, was about running fast. The current running boom people are more concerned with just the achievement of getting to the finish line."

Someone who goes from overweight, sedentary, or minimally trained to complete a marathon in six months (the typical time block for popular group training programs like the Leukemia & Lymphoma Society Team in Training) deserves to be lauded—whether that person finishes in four, five, or six hours. When you consider that the average American walks a total of only 1.2 miles a week (300 yards a day), covering 26 miles is an outstanding achievement.

My point about this mediocrity epidemic is not to discount the achievements of the masses who participate in endurance sports. I know many triathletes who simply enjoy the experience and the healthy, fit lifestyle and are not concerned with training fervently to shave a few minutes off their time. However, there are large numbers of triathletes who *are* concerned and seem to be pursuing their goals by training harder instead of smarter. A flawed training approach or a flawed mentality can render additional hard work counterproductive. This is true for everyone from elite professionals to beginners who find their escalating passion and commitment to training and competition derailed by fatigue or injury.

Consider the Degree Everyman Ironman contest, a PR promotion by the deodorant company to choose an everyday fitness enthusiast and train that person to finish an ironman within a year. The contest drew 3,000 applicants, with one lucky winner receiving a benefits package worth $100,000: a six-month all-expenses-paid vacation in San Diego (including salary reimbursement) to train with the best coaches, use the best equipment, watch the Hawaii Ironman for inspiration, and then attempt the Florida Ironman at the end of the year.

Any serious triathlete would salivate at the prospect of taking six months off to train for an ironman race and predict a vast improvement in his or her personal best time on the heels of such an opportunity. In reality, with a flawed training approach, that time would possibly be spent overtraining—replacing the stress of daily life with extra training and ending up in the same spot—fatigued and incapable of a truly outstanding race performance.

This is in fact what happens to many young athletes who make the transition from amateur to professional. Encouraged by outstanding results while training casually during studies or full-time jobs, they move to Boulder or San Diego to mix it up with the big boys and train full-time. But instead of escalating their performances to the next level, they simply become bait for the big fish to chew up and spit out in workouts. Often their performances regress and become slower than when they had a part-time, fun approach to the sport.

Veteran professional and popular coach Tim Sheeper of Menlo Park, California, competed as a full-time professional for five years. After enjoying world-class results in highly competitive West Coast races, Tim was inspired to take his career to the next level. He decided to move to Australia and train full-time in an elite and regimented program run by Col Stewart, father of 1991 World Champion and longtime Olympic distance star Miles Stewart.

The experience of total focus and extremely high-intensity training brought Sheeper not victory but exhaustion. Tim recalls, "I fried myself to the point that I literally could not even swim across the pool. My mind and body were completely shattered." Here is a very talented, accomplished, motivated, healthy athlete who crossed the line into overtraining and compromised health with disastrous results.

After a couple of years down under ("I had very erratic race results the entire time"), Tim returned to America and took some time off from competition. He got married, set up shop in the San Francisco Bay Area as a Masters swimming and Team in Training coach and started a family with his wife, Lisa. A few years into his full-time coaching career, Tim founded Team Sheeper Multisport—a comprehensive coaching and group training program, which exploded in popularity. With a lifestyle and career centered around the sport, Tim naturally returned to devoted training and competition.

This time around the results were different. With a balanced life, a healthy outlook, and a more sensible training approach, Tim's competitive results were phenomenal. Competing in the professional division ("I'd rather bat .200 in the major leagues than .500 in the minors," he explained) Tim's times were on a par with America's top full-time professionals. At the prestigious 2001 Interwoven San Jose Pro Challenge race, Tim turned in the second-fastest bike split among an elite invited professional field from around the world, finishing an incredible fifth overall. Today, on the other side of 40, Tim can still bang it out with some of the best pros in America.

Tim believes that his experience with overtraining in Australia has made him a better athlete and, even more important, a better coach. If you have that recurrent dream of winning Everyman Ironman contest, think twice about the effect of diving off the deep end of the sport and into a negative experience like Tim's in Australia. Instead, perhaps you can gain inspiration from athletes like Tim who make the most of their limited training time, compete at a high level, and place their competitive experience in proper perspective.

Tim reflected on his lessons, "I learned that you cannot rush the body into getting better. You cannot will the body into getting better. You cannot expect miracles or huge improvements overnight. You must treat your body with kindness and respect and come to the realization that this is your vehicle to move through life and you should not abuse it."

Thirty-Pound Racing Bikes and Hawaiian Sweet Bread

Next let's take a look at the history of the sport. Before it became part of mainstream fitness culture, a small group of folks, mostly from California, enjoyed a healthy, fit lifestyle that included rudimentary training in the three sports. Unlike other sports where performance standards in the old days are laughable by today's standards, people went pretty fast in triathlon antiquity. In 1982, Dave Scott won the

Hawaii Ironman in 9:08! He achieved this remarkable performance on an ancient bicycle, without aero bars, with no one to push him to a faster time, and with none of the modern scientific advances that promote better performances (heart rate monitors, performance nutrition, expert coaching and technique analysis, and so on). Update his equipment to today's $4,000, 16-pound racing bike with aero bars, throw in a pack of 10 guys on the lava fields for him to sit behind while they push the pace, and add Mark Allen to run beside for 25 miles, and his physical performance equates to at least an 8:30 and likely even faster.

Also intriguing is the performance of the mid-packer from two decades ago. Bob Babbitt, publisher of *Competitor* magazine, completed the Hawaii Ironman in 11:39 in 1984! An admittedly average endurance athlete, Bob's equipment, training regimen, and totally casual approach to the event were a joke by today's wound-up standards. More laughable was Babbitt's answer to my inquiry about the type of bike he rode. "I have no idea, but it weighed nearly 30 pounds."

Babbitt also achieved his performance without the benefit of performance nutrition, instead relying on seven peanut butter and guava jelly sandwiches and some energy drink to power him. Still, it was a huge improvement from his 1980 ironman fare of a Big Mac, fries, and Coke at mile 20 of the bike; a snow cone at mile 80; and a few loaves of Hawaiian sweet bread to get through the marathon. He finished the '80 race in a still respectable time of 14:56, which included time for a full-body massage after the bike ride. On haphazard, low-volume training and a forgettable bike without aero bars or other accoutrements, Babbitt was able to come close to the median time in the 2003 Hawaii Ironman World Championships.

It's logical to conclude that the performances are stagnant and possibly mediocre in triathlon. When an athlete is frequently exhausted, sick, or injured from heavy training, you can describe her

Competitor magazine publisher Bob Babbitt showing off his high-tech gear at the 1983 Hawaii Ironman. His casual training approach, 30-pound bike, and convenience store nutrition plan didn't stop him from posting a respectable time of 11:39. Experts speculate that he might have gone sub-11 on a 16-pound bike with aero bars, a Lycra skinsuit, and a more aerodynamic beard.

Credit: Babbitt Multisport Library

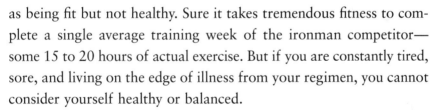

as being fit but not healthy. Sure it takes tremendous fitness to complete a single average training week of the ironman competitor—some 15 to 20 hours of actual exercise. But if you are constantly tired, sore, and living on the edge of illness from your regimen, you cannot consider yourself healthy or balanced.

When you are fit but not healthy and you push yourself to the limit in an event like an ironman, the body will often break down. A supreme competitive effort at any distance requires you to dig deep into your reserves and summon all the energy you have to deliver a peak performance. If the well is dry, your body will crack. I have heard more than a few stories of athletes reporting mysterious breakdowns at important races: vomiting halfway through the bike ride, back spasms, mineral imbalances, dehydration, mental breakdowns—all these weird things that "never happened in training."

Offering more support to this theory on mediocrity is the occasional amateur competitor who bucks this trend and performs admirably on little training or little experience. Sean Ramsey of San Jose, California, was an accomplished soccer player in high school, and then he left competitive sports during college and a stint in the Coast Guard. At the age of 30, he made some casual forays into a fitter lifestyle, hitting the gym a couple times a week and playing in an adult ice hockey league one night a week.

In the summer of 2001, inspired by some friends who signed up for a mountain bike sprint triathlon, Ramsey trained for eight weeks and completed a race of 500-yard swim, 10-mile mountain bike, and 3-mile run. Although 30 pounds over his high school soccer weight of 170, Ramsey finished in the top 10 percent of the field. Buoyed by this success, he caught the triathlon bug.

Soon he had a racing bike in the garage and had set his sights on the California Half-Ironman in April 2002. After successfully completing that event and several other Olympic distance events in 2002, Ramsey pulled the trigger to enter the Ironman Coeur d'Alene event in June 2003. This was certainly an ambitious escalation of goals, but what he lacked in restraint, he made up for in confidence and enthusiasm.

I put Sean on a flexible training program that allowed for his busy work schedule and lack of experience in the sport. Gradually he worked up to long weekend rides of five hours and long runs of two and a half hours. Despite the oppressive heat that caused a large percentage of the field to drop out, Sean finished the June 2003 Ironman Coeur d'Alene in 11:52. This time placed him a remarkable 301st out of 1,576 finishers, in the top 20 percent of the overall field. He also took fifth in the Clydesdale division (over 200 pounds) out of 106 competitors.

While this performance is certainly indicative of Sean's natural talent for endurance sports, it is also a tribute to a relaxed approach to the sport and a lack of chronic overtraining, compulsive behavior, or attachment to results. As former top ironman racer and popular multisport coach Paul Huddle says, "It's better to be 10 percent undertrained than 1 percent overtrained." To Sean, triathlon is a fun hobby, a refreshing athletic goal at his age, and a vehicle to lead a healthier, fitter lifestyle. These traits embody the ideal approach for the amateur athlete.

CHAPTER 4

HOW TO CULTIVATE A PURE MOTIVATION

Discovering Your True Motivations

There is a huge distinction between a competitive effort by a well-trained athlete and a struggle to finish by an ill-prepared or exhausted athlete. One is highly inspiring and respectable and the other is stupid. Many triathletes influenced by impure motivations seem to de-emphasize the pursuit of peak performance in favor of the raw accumulation of results—training volume, finisher medals, or one-upsmanship in competitive training sessions.

The only way to pull out of the negative influences of the rat race is to make a devoted commitment to a completely pure approach to your athletics. You may also choose to do this for your career, personal relationships, parenting, and any other area of your life to which you can attach a goal. When you notice impure influences float into your airspace, stop yourself and make a conscious effort to stay on the pure path.

Think about this the next time you head out the door for a run with a tickle in your throat, or step on a starting line of a race you are not ready for. It is this philosophical battle—between being a rat and evolving to a higher level—that you can apply all that wonderful type-A drive and determination to succeed toward. Be driven, focused, and determined to listen to your intuition, stay on the evolved path, and fight off the tantalizing advances of the rat race. Also, turn off the type-A faucet when it comes to the relentless need to accumulate results and push the body like a sled dog in the face of fatigue.

When one has a pure motivation and a healthy approach to the sport, there follows a natural and healthy desire to push the body to peak performance. Roger Bannister, the first man to run a mile in under four minutes, expressed this concept eloquently in his 1955 autobiography, *The Four-Minute Mile*. In discussing the reason for pursuing athletics, he said it "should become a striving to achieve more and more, not for purely selfish motives, but because of the recognition of some higher purpose. The aim is to move with the greatest possible freedom towards the realization of the best within us."

The word *freedom* stood out for me in Bannister's quote. Freedom could cover a broad spectrum of things that are restrictive, including freedom from impure motivations, peer pressure, ego demands, insecurity, and fear (of success *or* failure). For the compulsive triathlete, it's often difficult to distinguish between that quest for personal excellence and struggling through a mediocre athletic career, victimized by fear, obsessive-compulsive behavior, masochistic training, or other impurities.

Training should involve very little suffering in the true sense of the word. A program that emphasizes aerobic development, as is appropriate for a triathlete competing at any distance, will involve workouts conducted at a comfortable pace. Then when it comes time to push the body hard, you are 100 percent rested and motivated to do so. These workouts feel like an exhilarating challenge instead of suffer-fests. To me, suffering means feeling pressure to race for money or other impure reasons, or struggling through training sessions that are not appropriate because health and motivation are not in balance.

Ask yourself what your deepest and most powerful sources of motivation are as an athlete. Does fear creep into your attitude and behavior? How about ego? How about the need to measure up with your peers? Many innocent bystanders rightfully wonder what drives a triathlete to do something as "insane" as an ironman. It could be a relevant question to ponder. While an ironman is a daunting challenge, your motivations do not have to be unhealthy or crazy, and neither does your approach.

Fast Times at Ridgemont High

A simple way to remain pure and natural in the face of external pressures is to ask yourself a simple question when making decisions about training and racing, "Is this healthy?" This will help you cultivate an intuitive approach and serve as a brake for ego and ambition that can often run amok. Intuition is a blend of instinct; critical thinking and reasoning; common sense; awareness of one's mental, physical, and emotional state; and an ability to see the big picture of your life and athletic goals. When you ask an intuitive question like, "Is this healthy?" both mind and body must be consulted to determine the answer.

When it comes to workouts, most people take an overly complex and scientific approach, following a sophisticated training schedule designed to produce peak performance on race day. There are many knowledgeable coaches and trainers who can design sensible schedules supported by scientific data and real-world results. The problem is usually not in the schedule design. The problems come when other elements are thrown into the recipe—ego demands, obsessive-compulsive behavior, unbridled or misguided competitive drive, and life circumstances that affect stress levels. The typical result is a very busy, productive, driven person who is able to accomplish a great deal of work in training and in life.

These accomplishments often come at the expense of some component of health. Health should be defined broadly to include physical, mental, and emotional factors. A negative attitude is just as detrimental to your health as an inflamed knee. Many triathletes have the sense to stop running when a knee hurts, but less attention is paid to intangible health factors. If you train with negative emotions, they will hamper your performance and enjoyment of the sport. If you are anxious about squeezing workouts around life responsibilities, the health benefits of the workout are compromised. If you experience emotional stress when taking a break from training—perhaps fear of getting out of shape or gaining weight—your rest and your health are compromised by these thoughts and feelings. This is true in a quantifiable, physical sense, as mentioned earlier with Dr. Chopra's *Ageless Body, Timeless Mind* work.

Similarly, holding onto the past is not only unhealthy but can be devastating to athletic performance. Eastern philosophy harps on staying in the present as the key to a happy life, but it's tough to accept this truth when you get passed over for a promotion. Fortunately, athletics helps you experience the importance of letting go on a more graphic and powerful level than most other venues. No matter how impressive your career has been, it will not give you a head start at your next race. You can rest on your laurels, but you can't race on them! It's pretty difficult to run and hide from that truth after the gun goes off.

Trusting the importance of health can help you learn how to rest strategically. Often your fitness will improve when you choose rest instead of doing additional work. Most athletes do not have the awareness or the confidence to make the right choice in these situations. Driven by the rat race tenets of insecurity and fear, they perform more work, satisfying their ego and compulsions in the short term but compromising the purity of their approach.

In contrast, the champion athlete is driven by reaching her athletic potential. Every training decision is made with this ultimate goal in mind: "What training decision today will help make me a better athlete? What are the healthiest choices I can make in my life today, considering my goals of peak athletic performance?" Honestly, I have not met many people who embody this champion approach. However, it is within your reach—whether you are at the front of the pack or the rear.

After several years of training for triathlons full-time, I reached a point where I could not train any harder without suffering from burnout, injury, or illness. However, I still wanted to improve my performances because people were beating me in races. I noticed early in my career that I could not achieve the mileage totals of my peers on the pro circuit. If I attempted to put in big mileage weeks, I would crash and burn every time.

For example, let's say a top cyclist on the circuit like Andrew Mac-Naughton, Mike Pigg, or Jimmy Riccitello could consistently put in 300-mile weeks on the bike. Aspiring to ride like the top cyclists, I would try to hit 300 with negative results. Then I settled on 200 miles as my optimum number, only to lose races to inferior performances on the bike. I knew I couldn't do more miles, but I still wanted to get faster. Aided by my coach Mark Sisson, a former 2:18 marathoner and fourth-place Hawaii Ironman finisher, I decided to take a risk and alter my training approach to fluctuate my stress and rest more dramatically. On my best day my goal was to perform a workout similar to the best on their best day, but rest more as a consequence of my unique physiology.

Previously, my training routine would be to ride long on Tuesday (four to six hours) and then take it easy Wednesday with a couple of hours riding, an easy 40-minute jog, and an easy 40-minute swim. I decided to increase my Tuesday long ride from four to six hours up to eight hours and head to extremely difficult terrain in the deep river canyons of the Sierra Nevada. Tuesday became the day to complete my "Death Loop"—106 miles in the Sierra with 12,700 feet of climbing. The ride was brutal and pushed my limits as a cyclist. As a consequence, I decided to reserve Wednesdays to sleep in, get a massage, swim 15 minutes, take an afternoon nap, and then watch movies into the late afternoon and evening.

It was difficult to feel congruent with my purpose of becoming a champion athlete while kicking back on my couch watching Jeff Spi-

The "Corkscrew Wall" deep in the Sierra Nevada. This 2,200-foot climb in 4.2 miles came partway through an eight-hour loop with 12,700 feet of climbing—the ultimate Key Workout!

CREDIT: DAN VONSPANIELLE

coli order pizza to his classroom in *Fast Times at Ridgemont High*. The intensely competitive part of me thought I should be out there squeezing in those extra workouts to pad my weekly totals and stay in the same ballpark as the top guys. It took a great deal of trust to stay on the couch. In fact, at the end of my weekly conversations with Sisson, he would always say, "Remember, the key is *trust*." He didn't mean trust in him as a great coach; he meant trust my ability, my approach, and my intuition.

What happened was a huge breakthrough in my cycling performance and in my overall race performances. The year I implemented this strategy I won nine races, including the Coke Grand Prix/Bud Light US Triathlon Series and the National Sprint Championships, and ended the year ranked number three in the world. The combination of pushing harder and resting more allowed me to absorb and benefit from the challenging workouts and improved my health.

It is very healthy for a driven, goal-oriented, focused endurance athlete to chill on the couch frequently. And not only chill on the couch but chill with a completely clear conscience that your behavior is in line with your dedication to athletic goals and optimum health. One without the other is unhealthy and misses the point. Remember the old saying from Spicoli, "Don't be like the surfer who dreams about sex while catching waves and dreams about waves while having sex."

Hot-Tubbing in Sunny San Diego

It is obvious that you can learn a great deal from the training methods of the world's top endurance athletes. The performances of today's elite athletes are testament to the effectiveness of the training approaches that have been refined over the past 50 years. The first real breakthrough in endurance training theory came in the late 1950s with famed New Zealand running coach, the late Arthur Lydiard.

Lydiard is credited with being the first to evolve beyond the rudimentary training methods that predated him. Early distance runner training amounted to little more than circling the track at racing speed intervals until collapse. Roger Bannister recounts in his book how he allotted only 30 minutes per day for training, as he was a busy medical student. With that training approach, it's no wonder that experts thought the four-minute mile to be the limits of human endurance!

Lydiard introduced the concept of overdistance training and periodization for distance runners from 800 meters to the marathon. Lydiard reasoned that middle- and long-distance runners didn't need to develop their speed as much as they needed to develop the endurance to not slow down—maintain their pace in the latter stages of the race. Lydiard experimented with long-distance training, putting in ridiculous weekly mileage (up to 240 miles per week), and quickly became New Zealand's top marathon runner in the late 1950s.

He became an international coaching legend at the 1960 Rome Olympics. As an "independently traveling, unofficial coach" for the New Zealand team, two of his pupils won gold medals, Peter Snell at 800 meters and Murray Hallberg at 5,000 meters. Snell became the dominant middle-distance runner in the world, shattering world records with times that are still competitive today. Despite a relatively small population base to draw from, New Zealand distance runners (like Olympic champions and/or world record holders Snell, Hallberg, John Walker, Rod Dixon, Dick Quax, and Derek Clayton, to name a few) were dominant on the world scene for decades, as were runners from other countries like Finland who adopted Lydiard's methods.

Over the years, as the study of training theory intensified, athletes built upon the trial and error of their predecessors, and experienced coaches popped up all over the world. A few principles like periodization, overdistance training, and interval training became confirmed as the most effective and mandatory for any serious competitor.

Today, top endurance athletes in the world share these common principles. However, the variation of approach inside these broad rules is quite significant.

Even more significant is the difference in lifestyle between an elite professional athlete and an amateur competitor. If you wonder how Mark Allen was able to go 8:07 at the Hawaii Ironman or how Mike Pigg and Scott Molina were able to crisscross the globe and win over 20 professional events in a single year, you must get a glimpse of their specialized lifestyle. When one is totally focused and devoted to a singular goal like elite athletic performance, performance potential increases fantastically.

This seems to be a major flaw in the traditional approach to coaching and training. Coaches and athletes are guilty of ignoring external variables and following a training schedule that has scientifically proven to result in peak performance for an elite athlete. It is a safe bet to say that if you train over 25 hours a week, you will break 10 hours in an ironman, but the question is: how does one become able to sustain a training level of 25 hours a week?

The lifestyle elements required to sustain 25-hour training weeks preclude everyone but the most devoted professionals from attempting it. Besides the raw time consideration, a great portion of one's energy must go toward physical training. A career, commute, family, and other obligations of daily life all require energy that could otherwise go toward training. It is hard to quantify this energy, so most amateur competitors focus on the time element only when planning training and disregard the stress effect of training in the midst of hectic modern life. Most people can squeeze in plenty of time to train, but the natural approach dictates that you must also consider how squeezing workouts into a busy day, early wake-up calls, and the physical impact of the actual workouts all affect your body.

A serious amateur's typical training day may involve getting up at the crack of dawn to brave the cold and jump into a pool for a 6 A.M. Masters swim workout. After the session, the athlete rushes off to work and maybe squeezes another workout in during lunch hour. Then the athlete wolfs down lunch at the desk while reviewing voice and e-mail messages. As workouts are always conducted during "free" time, family obligations, oil changes, and picking up the dry cleaning are compressed into tighter time lines. The net effect is a stressful, harried life where one is always on the move in order to cover the daily to-do list.

A harried lifestyle of squeezed workouts does not jibe with the ideal athletic approach for peak performance. In college I took a course on the ancient Greek Olympics. The professor, Dr. David Young, was one of the world's leading scholars on the ancient games. He explained that the top athletes in antiquity were highly respected and extremely well compensated for their efforts. Typically a victor would win hundreds of jugs of olive oil, which he would then export for money. The value of these prizes made champion athletes among the wealthiest people in Greek society. They lived liked kings with servants attending to everything, allowing them to focus all of their energies on athletic training. Hey, sounds like the NBA!

Young advanced a thought-provoking theory: because this dynamic went on for 800 years, he believed that talent levels and performances progressed to the point that they were comparable to today's world records (adjusted for equipment and venue improvements, modern drug use, and other variables). While some may scoff at the notion of some naked Greek running neck and neck with 2004 Olympic gold medalist Shawn Crawford in the 200 meters, the theory is certainly plausible. Regardless, the dynamic that is still relevant today is that top athletes live like kings and have every element of their lifestyle designed to support their peak performance.

Contrast the typical "crack of dawn" amateur athlete's day with that of a typical pro on the San Diego tri scene. After plenty of sleep, the pro wakes up and leisurely heads out for a morning run, followed by breakfast and maybe some phone or e-mail correspondence or chores around the house. The popular group swim workouts are at noon. The pro triathlete pedals lazily or drives up to the UC San Diego or Carlsbad High School pool, swims a 4,000- to 5,000-yard workout, kicks back in the hot tub for 20 to 30 minutes, then enjoys a leisurely lunch before pedaling back home. Next comes an afternoon nap and perhaps a workout late in the day, then dinner, entertainment, and bedtime.

All-time great female pro triathlete Michellie (Mah-key-lee) Jones has been based in San Diego since she emigrated from her native Australia in 1990 at age 21 to make a run at the pro circuit. As Jones ascended to the pinnacle of the sport (back-to-back undefeated seasons and world championship titles in 1992 and 1993), she refined her training to a level rarely seen before her or since. Guided by her husband and coach Peter Coulson, a world champion amateur track cyclist, Jones lives a serene life centered around triathlon and free from distraction. She became known for taking more rest and putting in far fewer miles than other athletes, training by herself with strictly purposeful workouts, and racing only when she is ready to compete at top level.

One of Michellie's most legendary workouts is a track session of six 800 meter repeats completed in less than 2:20. Many top male pros on the circuit would have trouble completing a workout like that. While triathlon observers clearly saw her victories and maybe heard gossip about her awesome workouts, they didn't see some other interesting stuff behind the scenes.

"Michellie often stays in bed until 2 P.M. on the days of her track sessions," said Coulson. "We want to make sure that she is completely rested and ready for one of the most critical workouts in her training program." The thought of an athlete blowing a day sitting around in bed, sleeping in, watching TV, or talking on the phone may seem silly to you. Even among professional triathletes, few would have the gumption to engage in such a practice. But for the best in the world, the importance of following the path of a champion and conducting every single workout ideally cannot be understated. These

Michellie Jones's training program features less mileage, more rest, and tighter structure than her peers' but is strongly influenced by her intuition. Her sophisticated, focused methods have helped her enjoy one of the longest and most successful careers in the sport.

CREDIT: PETER COULSON

track workouts have helped Michellie outrun a lot of competition and earn a healthy six-figure income for over a decade.

It's easy to see that any comparison between the training schedules of an elite and an amateur is irrelevant if lifestyle circumstances are not aligned. Try this experiment: take a two-week vacation from normal life to train seriously. Go away from home and focus only on training. No work, no commute, no phones, no bills—just training and rest. In doing so, you will enjoy a glimpse of the daily lifestyle of a top pro triathlete. The difference in your ability to perform and recover will be astounding, and you will notice it immediately. This custom-designed, singularly focused lifestyle is what it takes to perform at the peak level. Beyond the actual workouts and weekly mileage totals, it is the reason why the pros go three hours faster in ironman than an accomplished amateur.

Again, the message here is not to stay in bed all day before your tough workouts. Unless you're a pro—then consider it! While Michellie's circumstances are different, it is critical to connect with the analogy. As Michellie says, "So many triathletes show up at races because they paid their entry fee, or because that's when they planned their vacation time. Engaging in behavior like this suggests they need to take a close look at their goals. Is your goal just to show up, or just to finish? Or is it to train properly, challenge yourself, and attain a peak performance? The races will always be there, but if you abuse your body, you'll soon burn out and never reach your potential."

Pears, Bananas, and Pasta Troughs

The career of former top pro Andrew MacNaughton illustrates the importance of looking at training regimens from a holistic perspective. The speed and intensity of MacNaughton's rise to the top of the pro ranks was perhaps unrivaled in the history of the sport. In his first professional season of 1986, MacNaughton, a part-time actor in Los Angeles, performed respectably in local events and was good for a 15th- to 20th-place finish in a national event. He was basically a nobody in a sport dominated by the "Big Four" and some promising up-and-comers like Mike Pigg.

However, Andrew was inspired during his initial exposure to professional competition and quickly evolved to a point where his life was fully devoted to triathlon training. All distractions and other forms of stress were eliminated until his daily life became one of eating, training, and sleeping. He lived alone in a simple apartment on a modest budget, ate healthy meals (usually the same thing every day), followed a consistent training routine, and, most important, embodied a positive attitude with a pure enjoyment of the sport and his daily lifestyle. His training regimen was consistently at a level of 20,000 meters swimming, 300 miles cycling, and 50 miles running—every single week.

The following is a description of a day in the life of rookie pro Andrew MacNaughton on the doorstep of stardom, circa 1987:

- Wake fully rested after 9 to 10 hours of sleep.
- Eat sliced pear and banana; prepare for run.
- Run 5 to 8 miles, ranging from easy flat surface to hilly trails (one day per week run 14 to 20 miles).
- Eat gigantic bowl of whole-grain cereal with fruit and skim milk, shower, and prepare for bike ride.
- Ride 35 to 60 miles, ranging from easy flat terrain to major mountain climbing. (One day per week ride 100-plus miles.) End ride at health club.
- Lift weights 45 minutes; ride 5 miles home.
- Eat humongous bowl of pasta (16 ounces) for lunch; take a two-hour nap.
- Wake up, and relax in afternoon—tend to phone calls and personal affairs, review previous year's race splits, etc.
- Early evening: swim 4,000 to 5,000 yards with national-caliber age group team.
- Eat dinner, usually humongous bowl of pasta with salad or steamed vegetables.
- Attend early movie; go to sleep by 10 P.M.

Note the absence of the computer, voice mail messages, faxes, e-mail, beepers, pagers, cell phones, driving in commuter traffic, screaming kids, arguments with boss, deadlines, time lines, and worry lines. After a little over a year of focused devotion to this training routine, Andrew had steadily ascended to a world-class fitness level.

To start the 1987 season, Andrew won seven of his first nine races, obliterating the competition (including the likes of Scott Molina, Scott Tinley, and Mike Pigg—the world's best athletes at Olympic and half-ironman distance) primarily on the strength of bike splits that still stand as course records nearly two decades later. Similar to Bannister's breaking of the four-minute mile barrier (sixteen runners broke it over the next three years), the leverage and momentum provided by the performances of MacNaughton, Pigg, myself, and others obliterated the mystique of the Big Four in a single year. In the ensuing years, a whole flock of new faces started showing up in the winner's circle.

It's natural to view this awesome training regimen—the soldierlike consistent high mileage—as being directly responsible for the performance breakthroughs that Andrew enjoyed, but it is dangerous to isolate the actual training from the lifestyle when making this conclusion. Many of Andrew's training partners who were aspiring professionals made this mistake and were buried on the roads and trails that Andrew traveled on his way to victory. It is natural to want to emulate Andrew's methods and hope that they predict success for you. Andrew saw a steady stream of young, talented athletes informally sign up for his brutal training camps and make their best effort to shadow his every move in training.

Some were able to hang with the regimen for an extended period of time, but the race results never materialized in the way they did for Andrew. Certainly natural talent was the major component in the equation, but I believe a huge factor for these other athletes was lifestyle. If their diets were not as wholesome as Andrew's, or if they had to put in hours at the bike shop or installing car stereos or sell-

Andrew MacNaughton's singular focus early in his pro career led to an astonishing breakthrough in 1987, where he cycled away from everyone and set course records that still stand.

CREDIT: EDDIE MARKS

ing televisions while Andrew napped in the afternoon, they were no longer following the same training program as Andrew.

They were attempting the same workout schedule with the deck of life stacked against them. Andrew's edge over the competition and his sudden rise to the top of the triathlon world was just as much a component of the hills he climbed on the bike and the laps he turned in the pool as it was the minimal life stress he created, the hours of sleep he obtained, and the nutrient quality in his diet.

Top athletes, from the ancient Greeks to today's heroes, live a lifestyle that is congruent with their athletic goals. This is one of the common denominators, along with periodization and aerobic base building, that all top endurance athletes share. Devoting total focus and energy to becoming a champion athlete is very difficult. While you may daydream of such a lifestyle, it can be extremely exhausting both physically and mentally to walk the tight line of a champion. Andrew's lifestyle clicked because he loved it and his motivation was pure.

It is important to ask yourself every day if you are having fun with your triathlon training. Every single workout should be fun and an enjoyable choice, or it should not be done. Even when I was a professional, racing for the groceries and the mortgage payment, the statement still held true.

Junk Bonds and Junk Mileage

These ideas may go against the grain of the type-A rat racer. In the workplace these concepts are laughable. The people who push the hardest usually end up the most successful. Remember the notorious junk bond financier Michael Milken? He revolutionized the financial markets by packaging higher-risk corporate bonds into junk bond portfolios that would become attractive to investors due to diversified risk (among many companies) and extremely high returns. He once made $500 million of income in a single year. Milken worked legitimate 16-hour days and was so singularly focused on his career that he lived a simple life with a modest home in the Los Angeles suburbs—no lavish vacations or other excesses.

His only luxury was a driver, mainly so he could work during his commute to the office. Once I drove right alongside his Mercedes limo on a Los Angeles freeway at 10 P.M. The cab light was on and he was visible in the back of the car busy at work. To most people in the rat race, he was the epitome of success—the king of junk bonds, a revolutionary innovator of the financial markets, and one of the wealthiest and most powerful men in the world.

Then Milken was busted for insider trading, in association with corporate takeover big shot and convicted felon Ivan Boesky. In the book *Highly Confident*, by Jesse Kornbluth, Milken admitted that greed got the better of him—not for more money (which he was too busy to even spend) but for the need to be involved in every big deal that went down on Wall Street. Even when the Boesky deal smelled fishy, he stayed aboard the ship and became entrapped in a highly controversial government setup to bring him down (assisted by informant-turned Boesky). He served 22 months in prison and paid $200 million in fines, the largest in the history of the Securities and Exchange Commission.

Had Milken been able to temper his competitive instincts, his world would not have crashed down. But Milken showed his true character by returning to the free world with a new approach. Today he is one of the greatest philanthropists on earth—supporting a variety of causes with hundreds of millions of dollars in endowments. Milken's influence spans to many cancer and AIDS causes, youth programs, inner-city solutions, and a large nonpartisan think tank for economic policy and human capital studies. He is a devotee of healthy food and has even coauthored two healthy eating/cancer fighting cookbooks.

Can you see where I'm going with this? A natural and pure approach is important and relevant in everything that we do. It's okay to want to make a ton of money and win big in the workplace, but it's not as important as your health, your family, or your honor as a person. You will feel more successful with an approach that incorporates health and fitness and minimizes cutthroat competition in favor of abundance and karma. Help others out and everyone will get ahead!

In endurance sports, compulsively pushing the body to achieve success simply does not work. The fallout from getting "caught up" as an athlete can be just as dramatic as it was for the junk bond king.

Witness the case of three-time Hawaii Ironman World Champion Peter Reid of Canada, who experienced perhaps the most dramatic crash and burn cycle in the history of the pro circuit. After winning his second Hawaii Ironman World Championship in 2000, he plunged into an 18-month downward spiral of severe overtraining and burnout—to the extent that the world champion actually considered retirement from the sport.

The downward spiral started as soon as he crossed the Ironman finish line. "I won [Hawaii in 2000], but I wasn't satisfied. I crossed the line thinking, 'that was too close.' I didn't sit back and savor the win. The next day I was already planning my assault for 2001. That was the beginning of the end." Reid launched right into hard training instead of taking an off season—a victim of the intense "more, more, more" vacuum often created by success.

In a 2003 interview with Bob Babbitt in *Competitor* magazine, Reid recounted his thoughts and actions during his decline. "My body started to fall apart," Peter said. "I was so far into the overtraining syndrome that mentally, physically, emotionally and psychologically I was cooked. I was done. I needed to get away and I didn't know if I was going to come back." It took Reid a year and a half to regain his inspiration. During his downtime, he gained 25 pounds and disappeared quickly from the top ranks of the sport, DNFing in two important ironman events in 2001.

By the summer of 2002 he was back, training with a refreshed approach, focusing on his love of the sport and emphasizing easy aerobic training. With this relaxed approach, he enjoyed a surprising runner-up finish at the 2002 Hawaii Ironman. Reid commented on his return to competition and his revised training schedule, "The love of the sport started to come back. In the beginning [of my career], I just loved to mix it up with the big boys. Then it got to the point where I was scared to lose, where I was more worried about what my sponsors thought than following my passion."

For his comeback, Reid sought advice from Mark Allen, the 6-time winner of Hawaii, 10-time world champion, and indisputably the greatest triathlete in history. "Mark's training was never complicated. He always listened to his body and did what felt right. He told me not to plan too much, because if you do you won't listen to your body." After a long and sensible winter break after the 2002 season, Reid returned to Hawaii in 2003 and delivered a resounding victory over a top field. Reid's third victory in Hawaii certified him as one of the all-time greatest triathletes. His story could have easily ended up differently. Even a world champion with top coaching and tremendous financial incentive to perform can go south when mentality becomes flawed.

The anonymous age grouper who quietly disappears from the sport due to burnout, chronic injuries, or severe disruption of personal and family life caused by an obsessive approach to the sport is not so lucky. We don't read much about these athletes or see their photos on magazine covers lauding amazing comebacks. Scott Tinley's revealing book *Chasing the Sunset* chronicles the struggles he faced leaving the sport that had defined his personality and his existence for over two decades.

These are the victims of an incredibly difficult sport pursued inside an already hectic and stressful lifestyle—a rat race within a rat race. Regardless of whether you are trying to win the Hawaii Ironman or just pursuing the sport as a hobby, a pure approach pays the most dividends in every way. There is truly no other choice if you want to remain healthy and sane while competing in a sport that is generally regarded as "crazy" by casual observers.

The Effect of Stress on Training and Performance

We have discussed the effect that life stresses have on your training. In this context, the word *stress* really means "overstress" or "distress." The distinction is important when you realize that stress itself is not unhealthy; stress is a necessary part of a prosperous and healthy life. Stress can be more accurately and pleasantly characterized as "stimulation." We stress our muscles and brains constantly and grow stronger and smarter as a result.

When you are faced with stressful events and circumstances, your body responds by telling the adrenal glands to release stress hormones into your bloodstream. These hormones allow the body to function at a heightened level, a phenomenon commonly referred to as the fight-or-flight response. When you feel that familiar prerace tension on the starting line, a host of things are occurring physiologically to prepare your body for peak performance. Heart rate and blood pressure increase, breathing rate increases, and senses become more acute.

This mechanism is a great help on race day, or if you happen to face a life-threatening situation. The fight-or-flight response has been imbedded into our genes over thousands of years as a survival necessity. Today it is severely abused as we live in a world of unrelenting stress and stimulation.

Your physiology kicks into fight-or-flight mode in the face of an intense workout, traffic jam, deadline at work, argument with a loved one, or anything else you perceive to be stressful. If the fight-or-flight response engages too frequently, the mechanism will soon break down and you will become exhausted. After flooding the bloodstream with hormones that enhance performance for a sustained period of time, the adrenal glands will start releasing less than normal amounts of these hormones that are crucial to health. This condition is best described as burnout. Physiological symptoms of burnout include:

- blood sugar fluctuations
- sugar cravings, especially at night—caused by low cortisol (a major stress hormone) levels
- digestive irregularities—stress hormones inhibit digestion
- fatigue at the end of workouts
- dizziness upon standing up quickly
- muscle/joint pain—particularly in the knee and lower back (low aldosterone levels)
- periodic blurred vision and/or eyestrain—adrenal hormones affect pupil contraction
- weakened immune system—susceptibility to illness and allergies
- insomnia, nervousness, irritability, emotional instability

There are many ways to arrive at that place called burnout. You can get it putting in high mileage weeks like a pro, working long hours and traveling extensively, eating poorly and drinking too much alcohol or coffee, or dealing with family difficulties like a separation, extended illness, or personal tragedy.

Dr. Phil Maffetone has written extensively about adrenal fatigue as a huge performance inhibitor for endurance athletes. The endurance athlete must be very careful about moderating the stress response in training and in daily life to avoid adrenal fatigue and maintain health while building fitness. The description of Andrew MacNaughton's lifestyle suggests that the only significant stress he faced was the physical stress of training. Training 25 hours a week is certainly a stressful endeavor, but it can be manageable and effective when all other forms of stress are minimized.

Burnout can be cured by eliminating some of the stress factors in your life, like cutting back on training, travel, emotional strife, or junk food. With extra sleep and a slower pace of life, you can usually bounce back to normal energy and motivation levels in a short time. However, the abuse of the stress response in the modern world often goes deeper than that and becomes terminal.

Immersed in the rat race, millions of people make choices that lead to an overstressed lifestyle. The consequences of living out of balance for years and decades are a shortened lifespan and serious disease. Numerous studies have linked the stressful modern lifestyle and hyperarousal of the adrenal system to cardiovascular disease, high blood pressure, migraine headaches, and immune system disorders like chronic fatigue syndrome. Stress is often listed as the number one risk factor for heart attacks.

Often you become so conditioned to your daily routine and lifestyle circumstances that you aren't even aware of how stressful your life is. This is particularly true when you consider that many forms of stress in your daily routine happen to be enjoyable. You also often hear the misnomer that exercise is a great stress relief from the pressures of a busy workday and family life. While it can be a great emotional and mental outlet to balance other forms of stress, it is essential to remember that exercise is merely a different form of stress.

If you envision the scales of justice with stressful lifestyle elements on one tray and restful elements on the other tray, the stressful tray includes your training schedule, work, traffic jams, emotional distress, paying the bills, and watching your favorite basketball team on TV. On the other side of the scale are things like sleep, meditation, yoga, quiet reading, a stroll through the neighborhood, and birdwatching. To perform your best in your triathlon races, the scales need to balance.

Remember, your body's stress response is identical regardless of whether you consider the stimulation enjoyable or upsetting. You may even lead a busy, exciting, happy life, but are actually under extreme stress. Consider that getting married carries one of the highest stress scores—simply because of the sheer volume of impact it has on life. The trick is to moderate your behavior so that the effects of stress are not so pronounced. With this insight, you can now look differently at how your training schedule should fit into your life-stress schedule.

Maybe you can't stay in bed till 2 P.M. like Michellie Jones, but you must continually balance stress of all forms with rest. If you get up at the crack of dawn Tuesday for Masters workout, wake up later on Wednesday and have a leisurely breakfast with the kids before taking them to school.

After extensive preparation hikes over the spring and summer of 2005, my wife Tracy and three friends climbed Mt. Whitney, the highest peak in the 48 states at 14,494 feet. This 17-hour effort pushed her to the limit and beyond. She reported that she had a great time but could have easily turned around at Trail Crest (13,777 feet) and had just as much fun. Afterward, she had no interest in hiking for several weeks. Tracy is not an endurance athlete, but we athletes can learn valuable lessons from her mentality and intuitive return to balance after her peak performance. Her focus and the rewards came in the process, not the summit.

PART 2

TRAINING PRINCIPLES AND STRATEGY

Chapter 5

PRINCIPLES OF EFFECTIVE ENDURANCE TRAINING

First let's establish some important training principles that elite athletes and extensive scientific studies have shown to be crucial to success in endurance sports, proven by competitive results and studies over the last 40 years. Regardless of what level of fitness and commitment you have, it is essential to follow these strategies as a foundation for your endurance training goals:

- Elite endurance athletes have an intense belief that their method is the best approach for their personal peak performance.
- Elite endurance athletes practice periodization.
- Elite endurance athletes possess and continually cultivate a strong aerobic base.

Training methods and workouts vary greatly among elite endurance athletes, even those competing in the same event. I will never forget my efforts to discover the secret to success as a young pro in 1988. I hit up Dave Scott and Mark Allen for training guidance when both were in their primes and battling for supremacy at ironman distance.

The opinions they offered were almost completely opposite, yet both were absolutely convinced that their approach was correct for them. Allen was a devotee of Dr. Phil Maffetone's aerobic heart rate training. He believed that the secret to improvement was to develop the ability to sustain longer and longer efforts at comfortable aerobic heart rates.

Dave Scott admitted that after several years of massive solo training miles, he grew bored of the grind and had to adapt his training to maintain motivation levels. Scott advocated frequent high-intensity sessions, strength training, and an overall strategy of maintaining brisk workout pace instead of accumulating long miles.

Periodization means dividing the calendar year into periods characterized by different training schedule emphasis. Numerous books are filled with intricate details of micro and macro periodization cycles and buzzwords to describe different periods—buildup phase, strength phase, anaerobic, aerobic, level II, level III, tiered micro-buildup phase—enough to make your head spin, even if you are an experienced endurance athlete! I believe that a simple approach works best and will discuss a general periodization strategy that includes:

- Aerobic period: emphasis on comfortably paced aerobic workouts/overdistance workouts
- Peak competitive season: characterized by frequent race-pace sessions and reduced overall training volume
- Rest period of reduced training

These three cycles can repeat themselves on a micro level too, always in the same order. For example, if you have a racing period of a month, you rest a couple of weeks after, then do a few aerobic weeks before racing again.

Do I Need a Coach?

Many people have come to me seeking guidance after coming off a disappointing experience with remote, dial-a-workout, online coaching. The problem is that the premise is severely flawed, and thus the product (books, magazine articles, group training, or remote workout-based coaching) is flawed. Attempting to follow a fixed schedule of future workouts is problematic unless you live a robotic life with minimal external variables. Even a top pro, whose life is organized around workouts instead of vice versa, must constantly modify proposed workout schedules based on variables like fatigue, motivation levels, weather, and a host of other real-life circumstances.

Coaches can serve a valuable role for athletes, but both coach and athlete should focus their efforts to a broader scope than just a workout program. For example, a coach can help the athlete design an effective training strategy where the athlete learns to plug in real-life variables and make sensible training decisions. The coach can even suggest a progression of workouts to follow based on certain variables such as the athlete's goal race and fitness, energy, and motivation levels.

Equipping a pupil with knowledge and reasoning tools and providing inspiration, guidance, and support—that is how a coach can be most effective. This can easily be done either hands-on or from a remote location. There are many good coaches who have positive, constructive, dynamic relationships with their clients. What I am asking is that you, the athlete, do your best to contribute to the relationship and make it dynamic. Draw the line at the point where long-term workout plans are force-fed to you over the Internet.

If you take a painting class, a good teacher will show you how to set up your easel and canvas, how to mix the paints on the palette, and the proper technique for brushing. But the teacher does not paint the picture for you. The problem with the robotic coaching relationship is that you let go of the brush and hand it to the coach. In doing so, you do not learn the skills or the responsibility to become a successful athlete.

Your actual workout schedule is of very little importance to triathlon success. It's probably 19th on the list of top-20 most important success factors. Your mentality and attitude, as discussed in Part 1, are far more important than the composition of your weekly workout schedule. The secret to training properly is to follow some general principles that will guide you to a sensible and effective training schedule.

The foremost guide to making daily workout decisions is your intuition, not a predetermined schedule. This is an extremely difficult concept for a highly motivated, goal-oriented type-A human to buy into. We have been programmed since grade school to follow carefully designed road maps on our path to success. Wanna go to college? Take your college prep classes, get your grade point average to 3.5 or better, and get a score of 1,100 on the SAT. Wanna execute the sales team's strategy? Fill out your weekly spreadsheets, log your phone calls, and expect an 11.3 percent response rate from prequalified leads. Blah, blah, blah. The problem with applying this mentality to endurance training is that life variables—energy levels, motivation levels, stress levels—affect your performance dramatically. Each workout decision must be made in a holistic manner. That doesn't mean structure is unimportant. You just have to have the correct structure that allows for adjustments based on life variables.

The following are some elements of a winning triathlon training structure. Make no mistake, these elements must be considered strict guidelines. However, they offer a holistic approach to the sport by allowing for plenty of workout variation within the guidelines.

The Base Vibe

Building an aerobic base is the key to success in endurance sports, because endurance sports are aerobic in nature. The aerobic base–

building period of the year is where all workouts are conducted at aerobic heart rates. Even outside of the aerobic base period, at least 90 percent of your training time should be spent at aerobic heart rates. This is true particularly if you are an amateur athlete performing below the threshold of human potential.

Pause here to hammer this into your head. Many athletes I have coached and lectured to have a difficult time believing this simple truth and an even more difficult time subscribing to it in training. The fact that an endurance event like triathlon is aerobic is not a hunch from Brad Kearns but a proven scientific fact. According to Dr. Phil Maffetone, 98 percent of your energy to complete a race, even a race as short as two hours, comes from the aerobic system.

However, many athletes come home from a race lamenting that they need to "get faster, get more power on the bike, improve my leg speed on the run." They feel compelled to hit the running track for intervals or push their body with high-speed cycling and swim workouts. Sure, these workouts will help you get leaner, meaner, and faster, but your training strategy must be placed in context. If your base is deficient, hard workouts will help you very little and come with very high risk. In contrast, with a strong base developed, you can benefit tremendously in a very short time from intense workouts.

Pause here for the obligatory automobile analogy (present in every endurance training book ever published). When you push your body hard with insufficient aerobic base, you are fine-tuning a Volkswagen engine. When you take the time to develop a strong base, it's like building a Ferrari. When it comes time to open the throttle in the spring, after a winter spent carefully building the aerobic engine, you have a much better platform to launch from. The Ferrari gas pedal feels different from the Volkswagen's—and it gets sick less too!

Now with your critical thinking engaged and counterpoint thoughts formulating, you may have heard that certain elite athletes or maybe even your local stud seems to pile up more anaerobic training time than recommended here. Here are some things to consider about elite athletes' training:

- You should never compare your own training to an elite athlete's or anyone else's. You can *compete* against others, but compare yourself only to yourself.
- Elite athletes are unique genetic talents. Some people can work harder, recover faster, and handle more physical stress than other people. Them's the breaks. Focus on the cards you were dealt and notice how *your* training affects *your* body.
- Elite athletes have years and even decades of an amazing aerobic base. As Dave Scott once told me by way of explanation for his shift in training strategy away from slow overdistance to race-specific workouts, "I just got sick of staying out there all day." This excuse is not applicable to many triathletes.
- Even super-duper elite athletes can hit it hard for only a limited period of time before shifting to a rest or aerobic period (or vanishing off the planet after winning a bunch of races). I have noticed that almost every amateur I work with takes less time off

A key component of Andrew MacNaughton's devoted training regimen was that nearly all of his workouts were comfortably paced. He built a strong aerobic engine without breaking down or burning out.

CREDIT: EDDIE MARKS

or is less willing to take time off during the winter than I did as an elite professional. Everyone needs time off, especially people with numerous stress factors in their lives.

When you are below the elite level, you can experience the most significant performance improvement by working on your aerobic function. Actually, a novice can experience improvement doing just about anything. If you're sedentary and you start running every day around the track as fast as you can till you collapse, you will surely improve for a short time. Then, you will likely get sick, injured, or burned out.

Veteran triathlete and Cytomax marketing guru Eric Gilsenan says, "Most triathletes experience steady improvement for their first 500 days in the sport doing any manner of training." In most cases, it's a "flatline" program characterized by a steady application of daily exercise stress instead of a structured stress and rest strategy. Anything works because the improvement curve is so dramatic from zero to 500 days. It's like the interchange between the two characters Mark Ratner and Mike Damone in the movie *Fast Times at Ridgemont High*. Damone, the self-styled ladies man, brags to Ratner about how women respond to the vibe he puts out in their presence. Ratner responds, "Damone, if you put the vibe out to 30 million chicks, some of them are bound to respond."

After you reach a certain level of proficiency (with chicks or triathlon), improvement becomes more difficult and strategy becomes more important. Many triathletes evolve their casual, fun workout schedule to one that is more devoted, hooking up with groups of "faster people who can push me." Soon, the once-effective program becomes too stressful and too anaerobic. Rather than steady improvement, stagnant performance, injuries, and burnout start dominating the picture.

The best strategy move for triathletes of all levels is to monitor their heart rates and emphasize aerobic training. This allows the body to progress steadily without risk of burnout and injury that comes from a more stressful schedule with frequent anaerobic workouts. The best endurance athletes are those who can burn fat most effectively and spare glycogen. Envision pulling some random American out of the buffet line at Circus Circus in Las Vegas to see if he can hang with you as you cruise through an easy 5-mile run. He would hang for a minute or two, then collapse on the side of the road exhausted. The reason is because someone unfit would soon go completely anaerobic (which literally means "without oxygen"— hence the collapse on the side of the road) doing your easy jog. An endurance athlete has the ability to continue for 5 miles, 10 miles, or 26.2 miles because the body has been trained to burn fat effectively during endurance exercise.

Similarly, if you were to try to hang with Ethiopian Haile Gebreselassie (the greatest distance runner in history, who once held every world record from 3,000 through 10,000 meters) at his marathon race pace ($\approx$4:48/mile), you would hang for probably less than one minute and then collapse on the side of the road exhausted. Gebreselassie is so highly trained (from nearly 100,000 training miles at a comfortable pace for him) that he can process oxygen and spare glycogen while moving at a speed that is astonishing to mere mortals. The goal of your training is to steadily progress your fitness level so that you can move faster and faster while maintaining aerobic heart rates (you could also say run farther at the same speed). The sensible and proven way to accomplish this is to train at aerobic heart rates.

Improvement in aerobic ability will carry forward into the anaerobic heart rates, because you are doing the same activity. This is true even if you don't do any anaerobic training.

It's also true that anaerobic training can improve your aerobic function and your overall fitness. So, if you have been training with indiscriminate heart rates and pushing your body frequently with high-intensity sessions, fear not. While you may be aerobically deficient and anaerobically efficient, you can benefit from initiating an aerobic base–building period and focusing strictly on aerobic base training.

After your initial and typically dramatic improvement curve, this is the next step to take if you want to progress with your fitness level and avoid overtraining, burnout, and stagnant performances. This is true if you are a recreational athlete looking to lose five more pounds or move from sprint distance to Olympic, and it is true if you are the number-eight-ranked professional in the world looking to crack the top five.

There are countless examples of endurance performance breakthroughs as a result of aerobic training. When Peter Snell followed Lydiard's overdistance program, replete with 100-mile running weeks and 22-mile-long runs, he soon shattered the world 800-meter record with a time of 1:44. This is a time that is still highly ranked on the world list nearly half a century later and would qualify him for every Olympic Games and World Championship final since he ran it! A strong cardiovascular and aerobic system will enable the body to perform well anaerobically.

Even a race as short as one mile will still be 50 percent aerobic and 50 percent anaerobic. I discovered a glimpse of this truth with my teammates on my high school track team. There was a dramatic distinction in body types and training methods between the sprinters and distance runners. We had some pretty mean quarter-milers that could extend their natural power and speed to race the 800 meters competitively. We also had some well-trained distance runners that could drop down to the 800 meters and race the quarter milers. However, that champion 400/800-meter runner trying to move up to a mile would get crushed by the distance runner, just as badly as if I lined up in the blocks for a 200-meter race. You can draw an analogy from this example to the amateur triathlete ignoring the importance of base training. As I discussed in "The Mediocrity Epidemic" section in Chapter 3, an athlete with an inferior base will run out of gas during a difficult competition. We were able to race the sprinters at 800 meters because of our endurance base; the sprinters could not race the mile because they lacked an endurance base.

Look at the Tour de France prologue time trial, which commonly lasts five to eight minutes. The overall race favorites are always among the top finishers. These athletes ride 500 to 700 miles a week, emphasizing seven- to eight-hour rides in preparation for the 24-day tour of 2,300-plus miles. In fact, you would be hard pressed to find any cyclist to match the Tour de France heroes at an eight-minute race, even the massive track cyclists who are all about power and speed. Forget about a 40K time trial—the best time trialists in the world are the stage racers.

The top swimmers in the world routinely train for several hours a day. Mark Spitz, Ian Thorpe, Michael Phelps—these legends of swimming competed in races lasting one to four minutes and set world records off of a heavily aerobic overdistance training schedule. For a recreational triathlete competing at races lasting 2 to 16 hours, there is no question about which approach to take for maximum improvement. Factor in your musculoskeletal and immune health (which easily gets compromised with intense training), and it's obvious that your most sensible approach is to be patient and build the aerobic system at low-intensity workouts.

Why am I pounding so many examples into your head? Perhaps because there is a disturbing recent trend among amateur athletes to disregard the proven methods and performances of the past in favor of intensity-based programs. This departure from tradition is fueled by legitimate scientific studies that prove intense training yields quick results in endurance performance. In my opinion, these studies, while valid, fall into Gilsenan's "500 days" rule. Anything you do with a novice or over a short period (such as during a scientific study) will result in improvement in fitness.

Peter Snell, who is now one of the world's leading exercise physiologist researchers in Dallas, Texas, is amazed at the abundance of anaerobic programs and offered some choice comments about the quality versus quantity debate in a 2004 *Runner's World* interview: "Even in New Zealand the feeling today is that Lydiard's ideas are passé. I can't believe it! I still hold the New Zealand 800-meter record—it's 40 years old. Most physiologists are trained on the idea of specificity and simply can't understand that slow training makes you faster."

It goes back to Lydiard's initial theory of endurance training: that the missing factor was not more speed but more aerobic endurance to *not slow down*. Lydiard was truly visionary as he noted not only the importance of base building but also the importance of a loosely structured schedule that favors listening to the body and personalizing workload and recovery time. Lydiard's methods are simple, sensible, and have been proven time and time again by the performances of great champions. Today, however, they are all but ignored by amateur triathletes looking to maximize the efficiency of limited weekly training time.

If you are still confused or on the fence, you can find interesting and detailed scientific rationale for this in the *Lore of Running* by Tim Noakes, *Training for Endurance* by Dr. Phil Maffetone, or *Running to the Top* by Arthur Lydiard.

The MAF Test to Measure Aerobic Fitness

You can gauge improvement in aerobic function by performing the MAF (Maffetone's Maximum Aerobic Function) test frequently during your training. You complete a measured distance that remains the same for every test and maintain the same heart rate for every test. You then measure your time to determine improvements in aerobic function. Because the test takes place at your maximum aerobic heart rate, it is not strenuous in the manner of the typical fitness benchmark, an all-out time trial. Nevertheless, you should only conduct the test when you feel 100 percent to ensure an accurate result.

You can use calibrated indoor exercise equipment, such as a stationary bicycle equipped with distance or workload measurements, a treadmill that reads miles per hour, or an outdoor course like a long hill for cycling or running track for running. You will then be able to notice improvements in performance by noticing a reduction in time over the same course at the same heart rate—80 percent of maximum.

My favorite location is a running track; it's simple and consistent. After a 10-minute warm-up, complete a predetermined distance while holding your heart rate as close as possible to your aerobic maximum. The test should last about 15 minutes. Depending on your fitness level, you can cover four to eight laps (one to two miles) on a running track to approximate a 15-minute test.

Perform the MAF test every three weeks and record your results. If your results do not improve, this is an indication of overtraining or some other problem with your exercise schedule. When you notice a steady reduction in time, this is an indication that your body is responding properly to your exercise regimen and ready to accept a more intense training load to stimulate even further improvement.

Once you develop a strong aerobic base, you can then improve quite dramatically when you introduce limited amounts of anaerobic training. Hypothetically, if your 80 percent running speed is 9:00 per mile, you could predict a faster racing speed of, say, 7:00 per mile. If you improve your aerobic function so your 80 percent running speed drops to 8:00 per mile, it's easy to conclude what will happen to your racing speed.

The more fit you become aerobically, the better able you are to handle intense training. Your heart, lungs, circulatory system, mitochondria (energy carriers) in the muscles, joints, and connective tissue can all withstand more intense training that will in turn lead to greater performance improvements. If you are doing too much anaerobic training and ignoring aerobic base building, you are building a glass ceiling over your potential. You will become stuck with the Volkswagen engine and get dusted by the Ferraris.

Here is a simple example from my swimming performance when I switched from an interval-based swim program to one that emphasized aerobic heart rates and stroke technique. Previously, I could do a hard set of 10 × 200-yard freestyle arriving between 2:15 and 2:25 depending on how I felt on a given day. This set on a 2:30 rest interval pushed me well into the anaerobic range by the last few efforts. During an aerobic workout on a 2:45 interval, I could cruise through a set of 10 × 200s arriving in 2:30 to 2:35 and remain completely comfortable.

Frustrated by stagnant swim performance and frequent shoulder aches and pains, I decided to dedicate a period of three months to remain aerobic at every swim workout. Instead of hard intervals, I paid great attention to lengthening my stroke and becoming as efficient and streamlined as possible in the water.

As my aerobic function steadily improved, I was able to do the 10 × 200s—completely aerobic—and get my average time down below 2:30. I hit sets at a 2:25 average, then 2:20, and finally, after a few months of devoted attention to aerobic swimming, got to an average of 2:16! My aerobic pace had now matched a peak anaerobic effort of several months before.

My improvement came about because I wasn't thrashing my muscles and joints with hard swimming several times a week. Training with muscles that were always slightly fatigued and joints that frequently gave me trouble (soreness, tendinitis) compromised my improvement just like the novice who goes to the running track and hammers every day. My stroke was flawed because stroke technique breaks down with high-intensity efforts and muscle fatigue. We will discuss this further in the swimming section.

With this steady improvement, I finally decided to open it up and do some intense training to prepare for upcoming competition. On my very first swim interval workout in months, I shocked myself by holding 2:05 for 10 × 200. Needless to say, I made a nice breakthrough in my competitive performances.

Oh Yeah, My Health

If you are interested in reaching your potential and enjoying your sporting pursuits, you must always place health as your number one priority. Most athletes put their fitness ahead of everything, with health as an "oh yeah" afterthought. When you are healthy, you are able to improve your fitness levels and compete successfully. When you compromise your health in pursuit of fitness, you will always pay the price in the future.

It might not happen immediately; there are examples of athletes performing at the championship level with poor health. Look no further than the pages of your daily newspaper as the lid blows off the scandalous use of dangerous performance-enhancing drugs in pro cycling, track-and-field, baseball, and football. Serious bodybuilders are some of the unhealthiest human beings on the planet. They are capable of fantastic workouts and are devoted to proper training methods, rest, and extremely clean, regimented diets of healthy, natural foods, yet at one recent show a pumped-up competitor collapsed and died onstage.

Unhealthy athletes may wait years or decades to experience the repercussions, but triathletes are a little different. Training for a long-distance triathlon puts your health at risk because the challenge is so extreme. Health must be the most important variable in workout planning. Any workout decision that compromises health in any way is unacceptable. When you push your body with a long or hard workout, you do it at a time when your body is ready to absorb and benefit from it. The body likes to be pushed, challenged, and stressed. Stress is healthy and natural for your body, but overstress is not.

It's easy to understand how poor training decisions can compromise your physical health (don't exercise with a sore throat or you'll catch a cold; don't run if your knee hurts or you'll get injured), but you must consider a broader picture of health when making training decisions. When you train under unpleasant emotional or mental circumstances, you damage your health just as if you were running on a sore knee. If your motivation is flagging and you force yourself to train through negative motivation ("get out of bed you lazy slacker"), you compromise a healthy approach to the sport. If you are experiencing stressful family or career ordeals, physical training becomes more stressful, too. This must be accounted for when considering intensity and duration of exercise. If you are pressed for time and trying to squeeze in a workout, the workout is unhealthy if it makes your day feel more hectic.

You must consider every single workout you conduct for the rest of your life to be a wonderful privilege not to be abused. You should strive to have each workout maintain or improve your health and well-being. Forcing yourself to exercise or exercising with negative emotions (when you are stressed about time or as an anger outlet after an argument) is abusing the privilege. Whack a heavy bag to get out your aggressions; hit the road to enjoy the beauty of your surroundings and appreciate the simplicity and rhythm of the human body engaged in endurance activity.

When considering what kind of workout to conduct, slow down and ask yourself the question, "Is this healthy?" If you have a plane to catch, a long day traveling, and a business meeting, your plate is full. That predawn run that seems like a good idea to your ego and your compulsive nature should be reassessed if you place your health first.

Andrew MacNaughton used to "taper" for his traveling days, because he realized that traveling is extremely stressful to the body. The thought of a top professional resting up for an airplane flight might seem a little wimpy (one amateur athlete I coach insists he is completely unaffected by transoceanic jet lag), but consider that the habit and behavior patterns of the top professionals have been proven effective by their performances. Andrew learned from experience that it was not healthy to train hard and then jump on an airplane. He would land at his destination feeling stiff, dehydrated, or otherwise compromised for peak performance. His travel taper became an effective strategy to both preserve overall health and prepare for peak performance.

Today my competitive triathlete goals have been replaced by the goals of maintaining optimum health and enjoying time with my family. I do a moderate amount of training but am careful not to cross the line to compromise my most important goals. In the midst of my professional career, a hard workout in the morning would gladly be paired with a generally lazy afternoon of reading, napping, and watching TV.

With a couple of children on the scene now, a lazy afternoon is not an option, nor a choice. I'd rather skip the hard workout in the morning and have the energy to run myself ragged in the park with my kids in the afternoon. If competing in an ironman suddenly became a big goal, I would have to reassess the various ways that I spend my energy and make the sacrifices necessary to devote the proper attention to my athletic goals and my mental and physical health.

It seems to me like some of the common choices made by triathletes are not healthy. Personally, if I were to plug heavy triathlon training into my current life schedule, it would be both physically and mentally unhealthy. Squeezing more into a busy life is never a healthy choice. Most triathletes have a lot going on, and thus the sport requires everyone involved to make sacrifices of varying degrees. I've seen spouses make monumental sacrifices and athletes become disconnected from their families and friends in favor of training. In such a seemingly unbalanced and unhealthy operation, I would have to guess that obsessive-compulsive tendencies win out over common sense.

A conversation I had with a "RAAM widow" a few years ago is a good example of an unhealthy dynamic driven by a compelling race goal. RAAM—the Race Across AMerica—is a nonstop 3,000-mile bike race from coast to coast. The "widow's" former husband was a competitor in the event, where preparation entails numerous 24-hour rides to prepare for the 8- to 10-day race. She described a typical family weekend as follows: get off work Friday afternoon, pile two young kids into the car, and drive all Friday night and all day Saturday at 17 to 18 miles per hour behind her husband as he completed his training ride of some 300 miles across the state of California. Sunday it was time to drive another 300 miles all the way back home. Whoopee!

You may consider that example out of balance and unhealthy. You likely know deep down when you cross that line with your approach to the sport and compromise the health of yourself and your family. Righting the ship may be as simple as training for a half-ironman instead of an ironman, paring your season race schedule down from eight races to four, or accommodating a personal or competitive goal of your spouse's into the family's annual action calendar. This is how you function as a team instead of as a self-focused triathlete disconnected from reality.

I've seen entire families become mobilized, bonded, and inspired watching dad or mom compete in a race and taking an active part in the operation. Taking the kids out to watch you compete in an event that lasts a reasonable time frame, giving them a chance to ride bikes or run around the race venue, having them row a boat alongside your open water swim workout, pulling them on a tandem or kid carrier bike ride—these are things that can have a lasting positive impression on kids. Through athletics, they get to see a glimpse of your character and enjoy the influence of a goal-focused, healthy, fit role model.

Iron, Tin, or Papier-Mâché?

These concepts are important to remember when you realize that various race distances and athletic goals have been established arbitrarily. The event organizers did not take into consideration your lifestyle when creating their events. The ironman distance became the pinnacle of the sport because a bunch of military types in 1978 combined three existing endurance competitions in Oahu and tried to do them all in a single day. The media got wind of it, the public saw the amazing and inspiring event on TV, the popularity and ambition spread worldwide, and the ironman movement grew to the monster it is today. The distances of 2.4–112–26.2 have a heritage, but they may as well be random. While the top professionals can make an ironman a legitimate race, for most people the distances are so daunting that just finishing becomes the compelling goal.

With precious time and limited opportunity to pursue athletic goals, you must carefully evaluate your life circumstances, responsibilities, and obligations to choose your most appropriate competitive goal. Aspiring to a less-challenging event that requires less training time and less physical stress might be a win-win situation all around. Conversely, squeezing high-volume training into your lifestyle can result in well-being compromised in the name of race preparation.

At the 2004 Californiaman iron-distance triathlon, I had the pleasure of serving as race announcer from 6 A.M. until the official end of the race at midnight. Over the course of this 18-hour day, my mind wandered to reflect on the following: What if the distance around Oahu was only 56 miles? (The derivative of the 112-mile ironman bike ride is the 112-mile "Ride Around Oahu" bike ride.) Or what if the distance between Athens and Marathon, Greece, was only 13 miles instead of 26? Would any of us be any worse off? What about our family and friends who wait patiently at finish lines or absorb the effects of long-distance training in daily life?

Several years ago, five-time ITU world Olympic distance champion Simon Lessing was asked why he didn't pursue ironman racing. "Why should I?" he replied. Simon had been a professional athlete for over a dozen years and had achieved peak performance goals at the Olympic distance. He has been rewarded heavily in many ways for his focus and dedication to being a top professional triathlete. In 2004, Simon shifted his focus to compete at the ironman distance. But that choice came when his lifestyle and professional circumstances dictated that this was a healthy and wise choice for him.

Am I ripping on ironman races or people who do ironman races? No. I am just as inspired as the next person when I watch these brave amateur and professional athletes battle their competition, the elements, and themselves to accomplish amazing athletic feats on the racecourse. I am simply suggesting that you stay in control of your athletic goals instead of blindly following the pack, staying up till midnight to pounce on the opening of online registration for that "must-do" race. Training for an ironman might be a little crazy any way you slice it, but if you take extended time off in the winter, make a pact with your loved ones that you are going to pursue ironman racing for just the next year (or the next three years, or whatever is appropriate). That way, you can maintain long-term perspective, sensibility, and balance.

Recall the careers of legends Mark Allen and Dave Scott. Dave skipped the Hawaii Ironman in 1985 due to lack of satisfactory preparation. He had previously won in '80, '82, '83, and '84. After winning again in '86 and '87, he pulled out the night before the event in 1988 due to a bothersome knee injury. Imagine the heartbreak of being the sport's brightest star, sitting in a condo a stone's throw from the next day's Ironman starting line—the brightest spotlight in the sport—with ice on your knee and deciding to sit out the race. However difficult and painful the decision was, Dave showed his courage and commitment to doing the sport honorably and correctly.

After Mark Allen won in Hawaii each year from 1989 to '93, he decided to take a year off in 1994 before coming back to win a final time in 1995. That sound you heard in 1994 was the echo of the screams of his sponsors and their six-figure ad campaigns surrounding their reigning Ironman champion. The same guy who figured out how to win Hawaii five years in a row knew when to take a year off. Imagine the inertia pulling Mark along in the direction of yet another starting line and the strength of character it took to make the wise decision.

You might agree that these guys had a lot more riding on their ironman racing than you do. But there they were, in the prime of their careers, sitting on the sidelines in Hawaii watching the event when the timing or their bodies were off. I know numerous amateurs who have raced despite bad vibes and bad bodies. Just because you have trained all year, spent a few grand, and used a bunch of vacation time to get to the race doesn't mean that you should race with a 103-degree fever. But it happens all the time. Never forget that endurance training and competition are supposed to nurture good health and well-being, not compromise it. This is true even if you are the best in the world.

The Power of Intuition

If I had to pick the most important word for effective training I would say *intuition*. Training intuitively will ensure that you avoid overtraining and make the most sensible training decisions every single day. I define intuition as a blend of instinct; critical thinking; higher-level reasoning; common sense; awareness of mental, physical, and emotional states; and an ability to see the big picture of your life and your athletic goals. The opposite of the intuitive approach is an obsessive-compulsive approach, where ego demands and other negative influences create a disconnect between mind and body.

For the typical triathlete, this is a very tough concept to internalize and apply. The driven, goal-oriented personality that you consider your greatest strength can actually become your biggest weakness. The trick is to balance ambition with intuition, and health with fitness, to maintain a natural, pure approach to the sport.

The desire for balance and homeostasis is part of our basic nature as human beings. When we get tired at night, we lay our heads on the pillow and go to sleep. We don't need to get psyched up or use discipline or hire a personal sleeping trainer—it's a natural inclination and a good example of intuition at work. Putting on a coat when heading out into the cold is a good example of a strong mind-body connection and intuitive decision making.

And yet, many find that a concept as simple as getting out of your own way and behaving intuitively is difficult to apply to a training schedule. Always listen to that little voice inside your head that knows the right thing to do. That same voice gave you the courage to choose the college that seemed right to you, say yes when the right guy asked you on a date, or buy the house that felt like home.

We all can cite numerous dramatic examples of intuitive decision making throughout our lives, both good and bad. I've talked to a few divorcées who knew on their wedding day they were making a mistake (ouch). Sometimes the reasoning or the process is inexplicable—you just have strong feelings for right or wrong. The power of intuition does not need to be explained to be appreciated. Get out of your own way, listen to your inner voice, and act upon it with great conviction. Let's contrast this with behaving instinctively. When my dog runs himself ragged chasing a deer on the running trails, he is displaying his animal instinct to hunt down the deer. He will run himself to exhaustion, never pausing to consider that he will never be able to catch the fleeter species. When a human triathlete on an easy training ride gets passed on the bike trail by some wanker wearing tennis shoes and gives chase, he is displaying his animal instinct to be competitive, to protect his ego, and to prove his stature and ability to all challengers at all times. When the triathlete instead cheerfully waves at the wanker as he is getting passed, he is harnessing his competitive instinct in favor of his intuition. He is saying, "Today is an easy day. Even though I and my $2,923 racing bike can toast this wanker, I am going to restrain myself in favor of my long-term athletic plan and competitive goals."

Sometimes when I felt like staying in bed, I used the power of my driven mind to get my lazy butt up and into a workout. Invariably, going against my intuitive sense to stay in bed was a mistake. As a reader of this book, I'll assume that you are a highly motivated, goal-oriented person. There is another population group that very likely needs to get their lazy butts out of bed to lead a healthier life. These people are not triathletes. If a triathlete is feeling "lazy," it's a very serious sign that training should be curtailed and life slowed down until a naturally high motivation level returns.

That said, I know that sometimes the power of inertia can keep you at rest when you could be out moving toward your goals. It's tough to get psyched for a cold, early morning swim or an evening workout after a long and stressful workday. At those times resolve to take that first step of the workout, then let momentum and inertia take over.

Sometimes I was truly confused about the best course of action in training relative to my energy levels, state of recovery from previous workouts, or fitness level for a proposed workout. When you pursue peak performance in a challenging sport like triathlon, you must continually push the envelope of what you can accomplish and with-stand physically in training. You have to get used to the process of fitness and realize that some days you feel top-notch and other days you drag. Regardless, the work must still be done to prepare for racing.

It's a good idea to balance your energy expenditure with your energy level. If you feel okay but not 100 percent, you do not need to stay in bed, but you may need to slow the pace and duration of your exercise. This stuff is not easy to sort out, and there is no substitute for experience. However, even a novice can quickly become good at intuitive training and avoid the confusion that plagues the majority of triathletes, even highly experienced ones. A simple commitment to listen to your own inner voice can catapult you ahead of someone with 10 years of experience who is driven by ego, peer pressure, and insecurity.

The confusion about training arises when the connection between the mind and body is weak. I have found simple visualization to be effective in helping me strengthen the mind-body connection and make correct training decisions. If I methodically visualize conduct-ing a proposed workout, I can usually predict how the workout will make me feel at its completion and determine whether I should do it. I factor into the decision my physical state and my other life respon-sibilities and then ponder my course of action.

For example, if I scheduled a 12-mile run on my favorite "Stage-coach" loop in Auburn, I would lie in bed and proceed along the route in my mind. Through my neighborhood, down along the railroad tracks, into the canyon on the Western States Trail, across the bridge, up the cutoff trail, etc.—all the way back to my house. On some days, I would zip through the route enthusiastically and by the end feel completely convinced that I was making the right training decision. On other days, even imagining running up the steep switchbacks would feel tiring and stressful. Instead I would visualize an easy three-

Former national amateur sprint triathlon champion Don Weaver runs the scenic Western States Trail in the Auburn, California, state park. Weaver never gave an inch on every workout for over a decade.

CREDIT: BOBBY JO POWERS

mile run, out and back on the railroad tracks. I would feel more congruent with this visualization and thus proceed on that workout.

Often during a run or ride I come to a crossroads where I can add or subtract time and mileage based on which direction I take. I stop right at the crossroads, reflect on my mental and physical state, and decide which way to go. Actually, when I'm vibrating at my highest intuitive frequency, I simply allow my body to drift in the proper direction without interference from mind, ego, or negative emotions.

We all have a natural ability to use intuition to help us find our way through life. I urge you to make a conscious effort to apply your intuitive abilities to your workouts as well. Trust that the truth to peak performance does not lie in a bullheaded, "no pain, no gain" approach. Trust that you are a driven, competitive person attracted to a sport that will allow you to learn subtle lessons about yourself that are crucial to your success.

When you become expert at training intuitively, you can use the experience as a vehicle to become more intuitive in other areas of your life—dietary habits, career, and interpersonal relationships. Golfers note: the same principle applies for a long putt. You can't analyze how hard to hit a long putt, you just step up and hit it intuitively. Your athletic career can be a vehicle for personal growth or it can mirror the issues, insecurities, and compulsions that play out in all other areas of your life. If you doubt your intuitive abilities, remember that we all have a natural inclination for mind and body connection, to

Dr. Diana Hassel of Ft. Collins, Colorado, 2002 World Hawaii Ironman age group champion, has learned that being more intuitive in her training allows her to continue to improve. "During my early years in the sport, I was definitely overtrained. I was always tired and would go through a burnout week sometime during my buildup for Ironman. I think people get into trouble when they start religiously following a schedule or a coach's training plan and stop listening to their bodies.

"I always put my intuition first, and the written training plan second," Diana explained. "I don't see a big advantage to training when I am exhausted. I feel like I haven't overtrained for any length of time for the past two years. I train less and perform better than I used to. Some of that is the base endurance and strength I have acquired over time, but I think a lot of it is the recovery that is now integrated into my training. A better diet definitely helps too . . . especially for avoiding illness. I do think that many athletes who are newer to the sport get in trouble since they haven't picked up on the intuitive aspect of training. When they try to do exactly what a predetermined schedule says, they can easily become overtrained," added Diana.

make intuitive life decisions, and to be healthy. Behind all the noise of the external influences of the rat race is someone who wants to have fun, feel energized and fulfilled, and live a healthy, happy, balanced life. The sport of triathlon beckons you with promises of this, and it is well within your reach. It just requires some awareness and devotion to a path different from the well-worn rat path.

When you factor in genetics, time available to train, life stresses, and responsibilities, everyone has his or her own ultimate athletic potential. Your goal is not to beat Mark Allen's record time in the Hawaii Ironman but rather to explore your own potential based on the cards you bring to the table. So while you can discard the notion that an 8:10 ironman or 1:48 Olympic distance performance is possible given your limitations, I believe that the average triathlete, with an intuitive approach, is capable of shattering the current performance levels we see collectively across the age group ranks.

Dr. Diana Hassel won her division at the 2002 Hawaii Ironman.

CREDIT: ELIZABETH KREUTZ

CHAPTER 6

STRATEGY AND SCHEDULING

Balance Stress and Rest

An oft-forgotten fact about triathlon is that races take only one day, or a fraction of one day, to complete. A triathlon is not seven days long, so there is no need to pound your body in training day after day to prepare for it. The goal of training is to prepare your body for what you will face on race day.

When I described extending the length and difficulty of my weekly "Death Ride" and resting the following day, I was increasing the fluctuation of stress and rest in my schedule. If you envision a graph like a Richter scale, the spikes went higher (longer and more severe workouts) and the troughs went lower (complete rest versus moderate training). This principle of fitness applies to everyone, not just experienced athletes. Because modern life is so stressful, we can benefit from more rest, period. Factor in endurance training and it's obvious that you have to build in downtime. Working longer and harder on a given day in return for an off day from everything is a great bargain.

In contrast, the working triathlete tends to pack his weekend with long-duration rides and runs, when extended blocks of time are available for training. While this may be an inescapable fact of your daily life, negotiate with yourself for a couple of Sundays off each month from both exercise and hectic life schedules. In return, consider extending the difficulty of your challenging workouts and then rest properly. I'll detail this concept further in the "Key Workouts Strategy" section later in this chapter.

Let's discuss some hypothetical training schedules for two runners training for a marathon with varied approaches.

Runner 1—Fred Flatliner
- Monday: Run 6 miles
- Tuesday: Run 6 miles
- Wednesday: Run 6 miles
- Thursday: Run 6 miles
- Friday: Run 6 miles
- Saturday: Run 10 miles
- Sunday: 0
- Weekly Mileage = 40

Runner 2—Spike Seismic
- Monday: Run 4 miles
- Tuesday: 0
- Wednesday: Run 10 miles
- Thursday: Run 4 miles
- Friday: Run 2 miles
- Saturday: Run 18 miles
- Sunday: 0
- Weekly Mileage = 38

Which runner do you think will be best prepared for a 26.2-mile race?

For a triathlete, the equation is more complicated than this over-simplified running example. If you muster up the courage to increase fluctuation of stress and rest, and intuitively rest when tired, you might freak out because you "haven't run in six days" or you "only swam four times so far this month."

Your concerns may be justified in a certain context, for the reality is that success in an endurance sport requires plenty of training time. The folks who are the best in the world do not get that way from a sparse training schedule. As Mark Allen once said, "The key in training is to do as much as you possibly can absorb, which differs from as much as you possibly can." I once told him this was this most profound quote ever. His response, "When did I say that?"

The more training you can absorb the better triathlete you will be. The question is how to absorb as much training as possible while designing a training schedule that prepares you for race day. It is easy to see that rest helps absorption, while pushing yourself with workouts that approximate the race challenge will prepare you for the race.

Triathletes constantly ask me when to train and when to rest. If you are a little tired, and a little busy with life, and you have a big ride coming up this weekend, do you head out for an easy 20-mile spin, or do you sleep in? The truth is there is no simple answer or formula that can solve the mysteries of endurance training.

I remember once having an extended philosophical discussion with my coach, Mark Sisson, about training strategy. Despite careful attention to diet, sleep, energy levels, and sensible training, I bombed out of a big race. I couldn't understand why some of the athletes I competed against were able to train a great deal more than I could, and I couldn't accept that I had overtrained. After extensively debating about my workout schedule, speculating about my downfall, and comparing and contrasting the approaches of other athletes, I became exasperated with the lack of a clear answer. Finally Sisson just said, "Hey man, life's a bitch!" After an extended mutual silence, I realized that he had just offered me the clearest and most satisfying explanation I could ever hope for.

Remember that glimpse we had into the lifestyle of pro triathlete Andrew MacNaughton? The day after a long training day (like a 100-mile bike ride bookended by easy runs and swims for a total of eight-plus hours of work), MacNaughton may sleep in, spin an hour over to the pool, goof around in the water for a few thousand yards, and then spin an hour home for a nap, followed by a relaxing afternoon and evening. This day, though it involved three hours of physical exercise, would be considered a "rest" day by MacNaughton. Those of us with real lives (no offense to pro triathletes around the globe) quantify a rest day differently.

I use the following example of my pull-ups to further explain the impact that fluctuating stress and rest can have on your training. After I retired from triathlon and didn't go near a pool for the requisite chlorine detoxification period, I decided to do pull-ups to keep my upper body in shape. Every day I devotedly hit the bar hung in my bathroom door for a set of pull-ups. I could typically complete 10 to 12 pull-ups before my arms gave out. Despite doing pull-ups almost daily for several years, I was still able to complete only 10 to 12 comfortably. Once on a wager with my supercompetitive childhood friend, Robert Benun, I completed 16 (one more than he did, or maybe it was the other way around, but this being my book, Benun only hit 15) and collapsed to the ground in total exhaustion.

Slightly frustrated with my extreme difficulty in reaching 16, I decided to see if I could make a performance breakthrough. I rested a few days and then hit the bar determined to take it to the next level. Surprisingly, I did 18 pull-ups quite smoothly—thanks to the few days away from my normal routine and the physiological stimulation of the 16 effort. I rested for a couple minutes, went back to the bar, and did 12. Then I rested for a couple more minutes, went back to the bar, and did 10 reps, totally maxed out. My hands and arms were shaking for an hour. The next day I could barely lift my arms over my head to put on a shirt. However, when I recovered a few days later, I could hit the bar and do 12 like it was nothing. With a single breakthrough workout, I had elevated my pull-up skill considerably.

I believe a single workout can transform a triathlete whose performance, attitude, and motivation levels are stagnant. A 200-mile bike ride I did with Johnny G is still fresh in my memory. On that day, I followed Johnny through unfamiliar territory, completely unaware of our eventual distance. When I realized during a lunch break that we had ridden over 100 miles and had yet to head back for home, I started to freak out. Would I fall apart somewhere on the way home? Would this ride overtrain me for my upcoming races? After all, I had never ridden further than 140 miles until that point. Bumping up your long ride by 30 percent at one shot is a little extreme.

Regardless of these thoughts playing in my mind, I still had to get home, so all I could do was clip in and pedal. After a couple of rough spots, I started to gain energy. In the home stretch, Johnny and I got really pumped, and we ended up time-trialing the final 18 miles home at 100 percent effort, just flying down the Southern California coastline on a serious endorphin high.

121

After that single ride, my perspective about a 40K time trial, or a 100-mile training ride, changed forever. I replaced the question of whether I could complete the 100-mile training distance with how fast I wanted to cover it. In races, my focus during the bike segment shifted from "Can I save enough energy to run hard?" to simply attacking the 40K all-out. I didn't worry where the finish line was because my frame of reference for a long ride was so far beyond the race distance.

You can see that the benefits of balancing stress and rest are mental as well as physical. Anyone who has returned to work after a vacation can vouch for this dynamic. It takes a shift in your mentality to let go of the belief that you must exercise every day or train a certain number of hours each week to maintain fitness.

Dr. David Costill, noted exercise physiologist, swim coach, and director of the human performance lab at Ball State University in Muncie, Indiana, has done extensive studies to prove the benefits of tapering. His classic 1985 study showed that swimmers can dramatically increase arm strength and competitive performance with a two-week taper. His studies with runners showed that runners can maintain or improve VO2 Max with a two-thirds reduction in training frequency.

Science has proven rest to be critical to performance, and any experienced endurance athlete can refer to numerous real-life occasions where he or she performed well after a layoff period. If you maintain a moderate amount of training, you will not lose any of the fitness you gained from your most challenging workouts or training periods. In fact, you actually make fitness gains while you are resting, not training.

Intuitively, your body knows this and thus sends messages to rest when it's out of balance. These messages come in the form of lack of motivation, low energy, illness, and injury. These are your body's ways of begging you to return to balance. If we can all agree on the sound logic, practical experience, and importance of the stress and rest equation, the reasons that athletes ignore stress and rest must be obsessive-compulsive attitude and behavior patterns, fear, insecurity, and ego demands. None of these are champion qualities.

Just as you need to balance stress with rest, you also need to balance rest with stress to maintain your fitness. Your body can lose condition alarmingly quickly with complete rest. The effect of three weeks of complete rest will destroy a massive portion of your fitness. When I sustained a serious shin splints injury while running track in college, I suddenly went from four years of intensive, year-round running to complete rest and frequent partying. After about eight weeks off, where I did almost no aerobic exercise, I proceeded to the track and ran all of four laps. My thighs chafed together with each step, and I felt uncoordinated and winded after a single nine-minute mile! The next day I woke up with stiff hip flexors. I was absolutely shocked at how my fitness had regressed in such a relatively short time.

That is the bad news. The good news is that if you have ten years or five years or five months of good training under your belt, you can quickly return to fitness after a break for illness or injury. In a matter of a few months (about equal to my time off), I was running at peak form.

When you consider the stress and rest equation, it is important to trust the magic of the body to adapt quickly to whatever you do to it. A day off won't cause you to lose your feel for the water or pack on an extra pound of fat. A week off won't do it either. Three weeks off might, but three weeks of returning to work can get you right back to your reserved seats in the front row. Make it a goal to become a world-class rester. Learn to unplug your mind and body from the constant pressure that an endurance athlete faces and trust that rest is a crucial element of your path to reaching new fitness and competitive heights, as well as better overall health and well-being.

123

Key Workouts Strategy

Key Workouts are defined as workouts that are difficult enough to stimulate a fitness improvement. A Key Workout can be a slow overdistance workout, an intense anaerobic workout, or a race—anything that pushes your body beyond normal energy expenditure and thus leads to fitness improvement.

I suggest you design your entire training schedule to focus primarily on performing Key Workouts properly. To follow the Key Workouts Strategy, you must enter each Key Workout 100 percent rested and motivated to push your body. And you must always completely recover and properly absorb the effort of the Key Workout so that your fitness will improve.

To follow the rules of the Key Workouts Strategy and conduct Key Workouts successfully means that all of your other workouts must be of the fill-in-the-blanks nature. You do whatever it takes to be rested for and recover from Key Workouts. All other workouts should be comfortably paced in the aerobic zone, geared toward protecting your health, energy levels, and motivation levels, and promote a balanced lifestyle.

Implementing the Key Workouts Strategy means you must reject obsessions like weekly mileage and the need to do some form of productive training every day—a major change in philosophy for most athletes. Instead of doing what your mind wants to satisfy ego and obsessive-compulsive tendencies, you will focus on what your body wants—stress and rest to reach higher levels of health and fitness. Additionally, Key Workouts prepare your body for race conditions much better than "consistent" mediocre training. Races push your body to the limit; you need to approximate these stressful events in training if you want to compete successfully.

Following the Key Workouts Strategy means your training log may actually have blanks, that the majority of your workouts will be easy and enjoyable, and that you can have a life in addition to your athletic passion. Vacations, illnesses, time considerations, and other real-life factors that interfere with your carefully planned training regimen are of little consequence compared to the big picture of ongoing successful Key Workouts.

My best season, 1991, coincided with some major changes in my training routine. I moved from Los Angeles to a rural area in the Sierra foothills of Northern California. I trained alone at a slower pace and slept more, and two days per week all I did was eat, stretch, and watch videos. I was insecure with the new routine at first—surely Mike Pigg and the other competitors were out logging more miles while I was watching videos!

I flew to the season-opening races in Florida and then to Phoenix, Arizona, to face strong fields. I had no clue if I would contend or finish 10 minutes back. When I placed second in Florida and then won easily in Phoenix, I figured I was on to something.

My weekly Death Ride came at the expense of a cute, consistent, and robust training log. However, when you develop the endurance to ride well for eight hours in the mountains, several things happen. It helps your overall fitness level, helps your cycling at all distances (as previously discussed with the Tour de France dudes), and certainly helps your run to get off the bike with bulletproof legs.

Scheduling Key Workouts

What does your schedule look like then? Well, one to two Key Workouts per week is the most triathletes can really absorb and benefit from. Swimming, because it is much less physically stressful than cycling or running, is not factored in here. You can push yourself often in swimming, but remember that stroke technique—instead of intense effort—should be your main focus in the water. If you find yourself doing more than one to two Key Workouts per week, reexamine your definition of Key Workout. It should be a workout that is difficult and challenging enough to improve your fitness level that you undertake only when you are 100 percent rested and motivated. I say one to two of these workouts because in practice you will likely not hit a key run and a key ride each and every week. It is important to view the Key Workouts Strategy from a big-picture perspective.

With the athletes that I coach, I like to go backward from the race date and plug in the Key Workouts necessary for peak racing performance. Let's say you have a big race coming up in 10 weeks. You will train hard until the final two weeks, so you have eight weeks of serious training to prepare for the event. I will highlight four to six key bike rides and four to six key runs to complete in that eight-week time block. Trust me, if you can nail 8 to 12 Key Workouts in that eight-week time period, your body and your mind will be ready to race.

This is a much more enlightened approach than plotting out an eight-week schedule of day-by-day workouts. Day-by-day workouts are not as relevant as whether your body is prepared for the challenge of the race. If you can follow the rules and nail the Key Workouts, it won't matter that you took three days off during week four for a business trip.

When I hear athletes speak of consistency, it is usually an example of flawed logic—a desire to be consistent with a day-to-day training schedule. This may matter to the ego, but daily exercise consistency is of minimal consequence to peak performance in a single-day event. The only thing an athlete needs to be consistent about during an important training period is protecting health, balancing stress and rest, and preparing the body for the challenge faced on the racecourse.

Now, before you shut the book in exasperation, let's take a reality check. If you were to pick your nose and watch Tour de France DVDs on the days in between your Key Workouts, obviously your performance would suffer—both in the Key Workouts and in the race. Remember Mark Allen's fundamental truth of the sport that the more training your body can *absorb*, the better you will perform. The challenge then becomes how to absorb your training optimally and how to target your race experience in your training. The Key Workouts Strategy offers a better solution than a volume-focused approach that neglects the important cycles of stress and rest as well as external variables like motivation level, energy level, and other life responsibilities.

You know better than anyone when it is time to push your body to a higher fitness level with a Key Workout. The flexibility of focusing primarily on Key Workouts allows you to train intuitively and sensibly instead of robotically. I remember an interesting article about pro cyclist Graham Obree of Scotland. Obree, who rode over 32 miles in a single hour to break the world record in 1993, was a highly unconventional athlete. He didn't race for a professional team, instead preferring to focus solely on time trialing and velodrome racing. (He won a World Championship in the 4,000-meter pursuit race on the track, too.) Obree built his own freaky-looking time-trial bike that included parts from a washing machine for only 100 British pounds. He developed a special handlebar and body position—the notorious "Superman" position—that hid his arms completely under his torso. It was deemed so aerodynamic that it was subsequently banned by the international cycling federation, and new rules were enacted to prevent further such innovations.

Obree's training program reportedly consisted of riding all-out for one hour on his stationary bike as frequently as possible. His quote was something along the lines of, "If I got on my bike and was too tired to give a full effort, I would get off and wait until the next day to attempt it again." He explained that when he felt fatigued, he *rejoiced* because this meant that his body was improving from the previous workout! I'll reserve comment on the overall sensibility of this training program, but the point to appreciate is obvious. Go hard only when you are ready. When you feel fatigue that compromises your training plans, understand that this is the process of fitness and adaptation at work—and rejoice when you wake up feeling cooked!

Picture a training week with only a few workouts that really matter—it drastically reduces the stress of needing every workout to be productive or meeting predetermined workout time or weekly mileage goals regardless of external variables. Recovery and workload are individual; it takes trial and error to figure out what's best for you.

Kenny Moore, the noted running writer and former fourth-place Olympic marathon runner, competed at the University of Oregon with Steve Prefontaine. After trial and much error, Moore finally discovered that he thrived on a program that featured one hard day followed by three easy days, while Prefontaine thrived on a program of three hard days followed by one easy day. A similar dynamic may be true for you and your training partners. However, many athletes get stuck in a rut, training ineffectively and developing self-limiting beliefs that they are less talented or less disciplined than their competitors.

During the miserable failure that was my college running career, I learned powerful lessons about individual training dynamics. I wanted badly to succeed on the team, so I attended every workout faithfully, did what the coach said, and gave my best effort to remain among the lead runners on the team. On Tuesdays we had our most important Key Workout of the weekly training cycle. We would usually run 12 to 14 miles with extensive intervals or fartlek efforts. It was a very lively and competitive session under the watchful eye of the coach, who would select only the best 7 out of 20 distance runners for travel to away meets.

Wednesdays were always a six-mile recovery run on the heels of Tuesday's effort. The coach would usually say, "Jog around the campus and look at the girls; take it easy." Out of a group of 20 guys, there were always a few who for some reason missed the Tuesday session and were running on fresh legs. Halfway through our recovery jog these guys would drift to the front of the pack and imperceptibly increase the pace. When you are a young, competitive distance runner cruising through your college campus singing songs and generally showing off in skimpy running clothes with a large group of other young, competitive distance runners, it is very difficult to drop off the back of the pack and maintain a sensible pace. To be a good runner requires a competitive flame that cannot be turned up and down as easily as your stove burner.

By the home stretch of these runs, the pack would be floating along at a sub-six-minute-per-mile pace—certainly not a recovery jog. I would finish the Wednesday runs fatigued from the effort, setting myself up for poor performance at the weekend races and overtraining. One year, our best runner was an engineering student who had afternoon study labs and could only get away on Tuesdays to train with the team. On the other days he trained on his own according to the program prescribed by the coach. For example, he would actually do a six-mile recovery jog on Wednesdays. Then he would come out on Saturday and kick our butts!

In my final cross-country season, I went slower and slower as the season progressed. By the end I was getting beaten by walk-on freshmen with no credentials, a final insult to shatter my dreams of glory when I set foot on campus years before. I was so disgusted with the experience that I stopped running completely after the season and just swam and rode my bike for 10 weeks. During the Christmas break, I jumped into a 10K road race—riding my bike 18 hilly miles to the starting line—and threw down a 33-minute effort that was 2 to 5 minutes faster than my miserable 10K performances during the cross-country season. When I crossed the finish line I smiled as if I'd discovered the secret of electricity; cussed out my college coach, teammates, and entire collegiate running experience; and vowed to someday write a book about it!

Following the Key Workouts Strategy will lead you to the training schedule that is best for you. Use trial and error to determine how much rest you need between Key Workouts and which days of the week work the best for important training. Always begin the season with an aerobic base–building period of at least two months. All your Key Workouts during this period will be overdistance rather than race pace or anaerobic training.

129

During the competitive season, remember that a triathlon is itself a Key Workout! When you implement the Key Workouts Strategy, you evolve your triathlon career from the typical compulsive approach to an athletic approach, where every step progresses toward peak performance in competition.

Heart Rate Training Made Simple

When I first started using a heart rate monitor in 1987, I immediately saw it for what is was: a fantastic breakthrough tool to help guide and control my workout intensity. Eighteen years later the strategy of heart rate training has become quite confusing for endurance athletes. When hundreds of articles and dozens of books offer new takes and intricate details on optimum heart rate and training, the athlete sometimes gets left behind on the street corner trying to remember which button to push to display current heart rate.

I think the basic strategy of how to use a heart rate monitor must be simple for best results. Here are the principle ways a heart rate monitor can help:

- Ensure workout remains aerobic by setting limit alarm at 80 percent of maximum heart rate
- Ensure that you have a proper warm-up and cooldown of 5 to 10 minutes at the start and end of workouts at 65 percent of maximum heart rate or less
- Ensure a recovery session by limiting heart rate to 65 percent of maximum heart rate
- Plan competitive pace by monitoring heart rates during events of various distances

Notice I didn't even mention using the heart rate monitor when you go anaerobic. When it's time to go hard, you go hard. You don't have to worry about heart rate as much as you need to push yourself and turn in a solid effort. Dave Scott says the benefits of an anaerobic threshold workout are similar at heart rates anywhere from 10 percent below to 2 percent above threshold. While it may be helpful to monitor your heart rate levels at an interval session, most people get too competitive and disregard heart rate data.

Aerobic Workouts

Your heart rate monitor is most valuable to ensure aerobic workouts. Because the perceived exertion at 80 percent of maximum is quite low, it's very easy to drift above without realizing it. Your heart rate monitor is the most accurate indicator of the metabolic effects of the workout, something that is imperceptible to you out on the road.

When you drift over 80 percent of maximum during a workout, a small amount of lactic acid enters your bloodstream. It does not cause the "burn" like an anaerobic threshold workout; you can barely feel it. However, even a small amount of anaerobic stimulation can hinder aerobic function for the duration of the workout and even for hours after the workout. Monitoring your heart rate is simply the only way to ensure that you maintain aerobic metabolism throughout your workout for effective aerobic training.

Warm-up and Cooldown

A proper warm-up and cooldown simply means exercising for 5 to 10 minutes at the beginning and 5 to 10 minutes at the end of each workout at heart rates between 50 and 65 percent of maximum. These periods on either side of your main session will allow your body to function at its peak, recover quickly afterward, and reduce the cumulative stress of your exercise routine.

131

A proper warm-up also benefits your overall energy level. Easing into your training session helps your body use fat for fuel during your exercise. Jumping right into strenuous exercise requires you to utilize quick-burning sugar for fuel, a metabolic change that is not easily reversed even if you slow down later in your session.

Taking 5 to 10 minutes of cooldown at the end of workouts to gradually bring your heart rate and body temperature down and shift blood back into the organs from the extremities reduces the physical stress of your workout and protects your health. In contrast, abruptly stopping your workout without a cooldown period can cause waste products to pool in your muscle tissue and even your heart. This can hamper recovery and pose serious health risks.

William Russ Scala, M.A., founder of E-Juven8 Program and an expert in nutritional medicine and cardiovascular research with athletes, commented about this phenomenon. "We know that elevated adrenaline and cortisol levels cause the blood to get thick—a component of the fight-or-flight response. Compression hemolysis (force of foot hitting the ground while running) also contributes to blood thickening as does the dehydration that is common to endurance exercise. This process can also elevate homocysteine levels, which can cause heart disease in endurance athletes due to the adrenals burning off all eight water-soluble B vitamins.

"Athletes can place themselves in serious danger if they do not engage is a sustained cooldown at the end of exercise sessions. Numerous heart attacks and dangerous blood clots are reported every year in athletes. Athletes with strong hearts—heavy stroke volume and low resting heart rates—are at greater risk of stagnant blood subject to clotting."

Scala continued, "During a proper cooldown period, the cardiovascular system is able to gradually reduce blood thickness to safer levels. Avoiding overtraining with a sensible schedule and attention to healthy lifestyle habits can also reduce the danger of athletic-contributed heart problems."

Recovery

I would like to define a recovery workout as one that supports your general health and fitness and does not compromise your recovery from or preparation for the more difficult and fitness-improving Key Workouts. A recovery workout has a special place in your training schedule and must be understood and carefully implemented to deliver the proper fitness benefits.

While a recovery workout can be classified by heart rate and duration, remember to always consider the context of your personal state of health, fitness, and energy when determining what constitutes a recovery workout. Recall the example of Andrew MacNaughton's recovery training day featuring three hours of exercise versus a typical amateur's recovery day of less than one hour of exercise.

Exercising at 65 percent of maximum heart rate or less constitutes a recovery workout. Recovery workouts are most beneficial when you exercise just long enough to feel energized and refreshed. A workout ranging from 15 minutes up to a maximum of 45 minutes in length for an accomplished athlete is a true recovery workout. As was the case on my college running team, external variables make it difficult to stay below such a comfortable intensity like 65 percent of max. Use the heart rate monitor to ensure your recovery workout stays on track.

Race Pace Strategy

For half-ironman or full-ironman racing, it may be helpful for you to understand the heart rates that correspond to proper pacing of these competitive distances. I recommend wearing your heart rate monitor in long races and in race-specific Key Workouts to build a database of knowledge about proper pacing. A peak performance provides a template for heart rate ranges that worked well, while blowing up in a long race can show you the danger zones to avoid in the future.

Unfortunately, there are no magic formulas for what heart rate ranges to hold at various race distances. Personal experience is the best vehicle for you to nail down proper race pacing. When you observe and record heart rates, you don't have to rely exclusively on "feel" to pace yourself properly. You can also maintain discipline in the face of external variables like the excitement of competition. (Remember the rookie who dropped the elite professional midway through the run at Nice, France, World Long Course because the pace "felt" too slow!)

CHAPTER 7

DISPELLING POPULAR TRIATHLON STRATEGIES

The Myth of Speed Work

Let's face it, triathletes—even the best—go relatively slow in every sport. Speed workouts are of extremely minimal importance to success in triathlon. This is particularly true if you are not an elite athlete. Workouts conducted at anaerobic heart rates provide minimal benefit in exchange for a large amount of energy cost. Conducting frequent high-intensity workouts is an inefficient way to improve as a triathlete and comes with a high risk of overtraining, burnout, and injury.

Building an aerobic base is the most important physical training concept in endurance sports, and yet aerobic training is horribly ignored and disrespected by amateur triathletes across the globe. Why? Perhaps a compulsive mentality steers triathletes toward intense training. These workouts provide instant gratification as an adrenaline rush and a sense of accomplishment, offer a competitive outlet, and seem "time efficient" to the time-stressed athlete hoping to improve fitness levels. If you have only one hour a day to train, why not go hard to maximize the training effect? Especially when numerous magazine articles and even experienced coaches suggest it! If you are new to endurance sports, you may be inclined to push your body too hard out of fear and insecurity.

That said, speed workouts can deliver huge benefits under the right circumstances, namely for an athlete with a strong aerobic base who is 100 percent rested and motivated to push hard. If you want to drop from 1:52 to 1:48 at Olympic distance (the difference between making a living as a top pro and going hungry in seventh place), properly conducted speed workouts may be the ticket to your breakthrough. Someone who can go 1:52 for Olympic distance possesses a substantial aerobic base—a prerequisite for conducting intense anaerobic training. But in the big picture, speed workouts are still of minimal importance. The big challenge is to get down to 1:52 by becoming a great endurance athlete. Shaving those last few minutes off is like painting window trim after building a house.

If you want to drop from 2:30 to 2:15, or from 2:15 to 2:05, at Olympic distance, or go under 10, 11, 12, or 13 hours in an ironman, almost all of your focus should be on the development of your aerobic system. As discussed in the "Key Workouts Strategy" section in Chapter 6, you should focus primarily on aerobic overdistance Key Workouts—long rides and runs that build your body's aerobic energy systems and make you efficient at long-distance endurance events. Once you feel super strong during the last hour of a five-hour training ride in the hills and are able to recover quickly, then you can consider introducing anaerobic work into your training to experience additional improvement.

Training at or faster than race pace will obviously adapt your body to racing. However, this simple truth has been distorted by athletes and coaches because they ignore other variables. When I was a high school runner training 20 to 40 miles per week, I read a book describing the training methods of the top high school runners in history.

One national record holder ran an easy eight miles every morning in the mountains, then attended track practice with his team in the afternoon. How simple! Just add an eight-miler before school and I'll dominate. The next morning, off went my alarm and I headed out into the darkness for an eight-miler before school. By second period, I had dozed off at my desk and awoke to the shrill voice of my English teacher, Mrs. Feldman, ridiculing me in front of the whole class.

I was sent to the principal's office, with Mrs. Feldman muttering drug use innuendo under her breath. Luckily, the principal was a track fan and let me off the hook. When I checked in for afternoon track practice, I was licking a double-scoop ice cream cone and bidding farewell to the runners heading off for their training session. The moral of the story? You can't just plug into some arbitrary winning training schedule that easily. Since I did not have the base or durability of a national record holder, his schedule was irrelevant to me, and my legs had no more miles in them that day.

Similarly, the scientific studies showing the importance of speed workouts and the many books, articles, and coaches advocating them use flawed logic. If you walk into a laboratory as an untrained, moderately trained, or even well-trained endurance athlete and bang out anaerobic workouts for six weeks, you will likely improve much more than doing comfortable base training for six weeks. If you had only six weeks to continue your career and a peak performance at the end of that time, by all means hammer out some race pace workouts to perform your best.

If you want to take a long-term, holistic approach to your triathlon career, understand how anaerobic training is a small piece of the puzzle. Courtney Polakovic, a former national-caliber marathon runner, calls anaerobic training "dynamite." If used properly, it can deliver explosive results. If mishandled, it can blow you up!

The big problem that occurs when aerobic base building is not emphasized and too much anaerobic training is undertaken is that you do not become good at burning fat, which is the key to success in an endurance event. One of the characteristics of anaerobic metabolism is that you burn a greater percentage of sugar (glucose) to fat than you would during an aerobic workout or at rest, where fat is typically the preferred fuel source. (Aerobic literally means "with oxygen," and oxygen is necessary to metabolize fat.) When your pace escalates into anaerobic range, your muscles have insufficient oxygen to burn, and glucose (which burns better without oxygen) becomes your primary energy source.

According to Dr. Phil Maffetone, when you conduct an intense anaerobic workout, the percentage of sugar to fat that you burn can increase dramatically. This happens not only during the workout, but for up to 24 hours after the session (depending on your particular metabolic factors). The "hours after" part comes because a workout has such an intense effect on your metabolism and other body systems. With your cardiovascular system working two to three times harder than at rest, that hour workout has a more profound effect on your body than many hours of rest, obviously.

In simplified terms, excessive anaerobic workouts without an aerobic base make you good at burning sugar—all the time. This is the reason why millions of devoted exercisers who watch their diet and hit the gym for step or Spinning class several times per week can't seem to lose excess body fat. When exercisers go beyond their aerobic maximum heart rate at nearly every workout, they do not become efficient at burning fat. Instead they develop intense cravings for sugar after workouts and in the evening. The 600 calories they burn at Spinning class get matched by the ice cream and potato chips in front of the TV that night.

This dynamic is not limited to the beginner in the window at the gym. Accomplished endurance athletes who ignore this principle will find themselves with 5 to 10 pounds of extra body fat, frequent fatigue, a diet laden with too much sugar (due to cravings brought about by training depletion), illness, injury, and mediocre performance in competition despite hard training. In contrast, aerobic training teaches your body to efficiently burn fat around the clock. Fit endurance athletes are able to maintain low body fat levels (even when they eat a ton!) because they are so good at burning fat—a product of a successful aerobic base.

Stress and Rest for 18-Inch Guns

It's common for triathletes to try to balance their schedules with a mix of different workouts—long runs and rides, track workouts, cycling intervals, and so on. This approach compromises development in all areas because your workouts are not specific and focused. The ripped physique of a bodybuilder with those 18-inch biceps comes not from a daily regimen of working all body parts but from a very specialized program that follows the natural law of stress + rest = adaptation. The bodybuilder isolates body parts at every workout and integrates extensive rest for a particular body part between challenging sessions. Yes, the daily regimen of 20 egg whites, 80 vitamin pills, and anabolic steroid injections help too, but the example is highly relevant—specificity of training is critical to improving beyond the novice level.

If you drop swimming and running and focus all of your efforts on cycling, you will become a vastly superior cyclist. If you drop speed work for a period of time (periodization) and focus on aerobic base building, you will develop your aerobic system optimally.

When it comes time for anaerobic workouts in preparation for intense racing, you eliminate all overdistance workouts and slash total weekly workout time. This allows you to apply all of your energy to some very intense workouts, at certain times of the year and following strict guidelines. With all these factors in place you will experience the amazing fitness and body composition benefits that come from intense anaerobic workouts, and you will no longer take an intellectual backseat to your friendly neighborhood bodybuilder.

Accosting the Grip

Aerobic base building is not some new theory cooked up by Brad Kearns to sell books. This is a time-tested truth of endurance sports, as proven by the training methods of world-record holders in every endurance event. I opened my eyes to the truth in 1988 when I accosted Mark Allen at the finish line of an early-season race. Mark was the world's dominant athlete and obviously on an entirely different level from me and nearly every other competitive professional.

I'd just finished a very disappointing race, on the heels of the most intense and challenging training period of my life. I trained as hard as I possibly could, was sore and tired most of the time, and had just been toasted on the racecourse. I went up to Allen and asked him point-blank, "What's going on? What are you doing?" He graciously explained the evolution of his training program and the essential secrets of the sport during our casual finish line conversation.

Make no mistake, Allen was a superhuman talent and experienced immediate success at the highest levels of the sport, winning the Nice, France, World Long Course Championships in his first year as a pro. However, his first several years in the sport were tainted by frequent injuries as he struggled to maintain the high mileage standards of volume kings Scott Tinley and Scott Molina. While his nickname, "Grip of Death," came from his penchant for making people suffer on the bike in training (you took a death grip on the handlebars when you rode with him), Allen paid a price for his intense regimen.

Guided by Maffetone, the revolutionary endurance coach and author, Allen shifted his training emphasis from Grip of Death to aerobic base building. In doing so he preserved his health (both immune system and skeletal), strengthened his cardiovascular system and connective tissue, and improved his ability to burn fat. When the time came for anaerobic training and racing, his body was better able to absorb and benefit from the Grip of Death sessions. The year after our discussion Allen won the first of his six Hawaii Ironman titles,

Mark Allen—the "Grip of Death"—figured out the sport better than anyone. His dominant performances at all distances qualify him as one of the greatest endurance athletes in history.

CREDIT: LOIS SCHWARTZ

smashing the course record with his 8:09 performance in the epic duel with Dave Scott. In interviews about his breakthrough victory, Allen credited his aerobic improvement, which enabled him to extend his training days and long workouts. His message, paraphrased, was, "Taking a long day from five or six hours up to eight or nine is the best way to prepare for an eight-hour race."

Pigg Power

The Mike Pigg story is equally dramatic. Pigg may be the greatest Olympic distance triathlete in history. His cycling performances in the late 1980s and early '90s have yet to be equaled and possibly never will be with the new emphasis on drafting legal ITU racing. In 1986, Pigg exploded on the scene and started turning in bike splits that were out of reach of the entire pro field, allowing him to coast to easy victories week after week.

In '88, Pigg won 15 of 20 races and took second place at Hawaii Ironman. He started the year with what I consider the best cycling performance in the history of the sport. At the nationally televised,

$100,000-plus prize purse America's Paradise half-ironman triathlon on the Caribbean island of St. Croix, Pigg amassed a 13-minute lead off the bike against one of the best international fields ever assembled. Following him off the bike were hacks like Lance Armstrong, Mark Allen, and Andrew MacNaughton.

Pigg's 2:16 split (average of 25 miles per hour) over a hot, hilly, poorly paved, twisty-turny route replete with the "Beast"—a 700-foot ascent in a single mile (which knocked .6 miles per hour off his average speed)—was superhuman. Pigg's combination of prolific short course dominance and elite placing in Hawaii made him seem indestructible and unbeatable. Alas, Pigg started to feel human in 1989, struggling with food poisoning and other maladies. Mark Allen got the better of him on the short course en route to his undefeated season, and he bombed out in ultradistance attempts. By the end of the year, Pigg remembers, "I was completely burnt out. I'd raced like crazy for several years all over the globe. I had pushed myself extremely hard with high-mileage, high-intensity workouts, often alone in Arcata, California [his hometown]. I really thought my career was nearing an end because I simply could not push anymore."

After consultation with Dr. Maffetone, Pigg decided to commence the 1990 season with gentle aerobic training only. Under "doctor's orders," Pigg spent 100 percent of his workouts during the first five months of the year at heart rates of 155 beats per minute or less, ensuring that his workouts were completely aerobic in nature. His health and energy levels began to improve. Over the next two years, Pigg conducted the great majority of his workouts at aerobic heart rates, "racing off of base" and enjoying fantastic results. As his health and energy levels improved, Pigg gradually reintroduced anaerobic workouts into his training schedule.

Unlike the typical calendar-obsessed robotic approach to intense workouts, Pigg instead explained the intuitive nature of his efforts. "I would naturally decide to go hard about two to three times per month," explained Pigg. "Once in a while I just needed to see what

I had, but it was hard to predict when those days would be. It was all based on intuition. I wish I had discovered these methods earlier in my career. Switching to aerobic emphasis literally added seven years to the length of my career," added Pigg.

His 1991 season with 9 victories in 11 races was perhaps the best of his career. Pigg actually improved his running speed substantially in '90–'91, despite dramatically reducing the overall intensity level of his training. Skeptics who wonder how you can race fast if you train slowly need only look at this dramatic evidence from the two top athletes in the history of the sport.

Pigg conducted regular time trials to assess improvements in aerobic function. At the beginning of his aerobic training period, he completed five miles in 33:00, with an average speed of 6:33 per mile. Over time Pigg improved his five-mile time trial to a 28:36—a phenomenal 5:43 per mile at only around 80 percent of maximum effort! This is the essence of how to improve in an endurance sport like triathlon. Rather than slamming out intervals at your goal race pace, you back into the solution by steadily improving your speed at conversational aerobic pace.

Crash and burn with excessive intensity or steadily improve with an aerobic emphasis—the choice is obvious. Since you may not have a chance to accost Mark Allen at a finish line soon, I'll let you in on a little secret: this sport does not have to be about suffering, injuries, and fatigue. Intense anaerobic workouts will contribute minimally to your improvement and, if abused, will be the primary cause of your downfall. Almost every workout you do should be enjoyable and comfortable, both physically and mentally. This is true even when it is time to push yourself and go hard or long. When the time is right, your body is rested and well prepared, and your mind is eager for the challenge. Intense workouts and races should be positive experiences, even if they are painful. As Lance Armstrong said, "Suffering on the bike makes me feel alive." If the suffering was daily (as reflected in many faces in the health club), we would likely sing a different tune!

Mike Pigg's career took off in remote Arcata, California. He conquered the sport his way, with a superhuman work ethic and a constant quest for new challenges and personal improvement. If you think you are training hard, you should first view some of Pigg's workout logs from the late 1980s.

CREDIT: MIKE PIGG

Having a high motivation to train and a positive attitude toward your workouts are your greatest weapons. They must always be present. If they are not present, your workout will probably not benefit you in any way, on or off the racecourse. Enjoy life, eat healthy food, live in balance, attack your goals with great enthusiasm and energy, always do your best, put your health first, and choose a positive attitude and a pure motivation—a long sentence but a very concise formula for success in triathlons and in life.

Feel the Burn

Anaerobic workouts produce awesome benefits because they challenge you to break through to a higher fitness level. When you put the body under stress and recover from that stress properly, it will adapt and become stronger. As discussed previously, these workouts are highly volatile and must be conducted under the strictest guidelines. I call these guidelines my **Four Rules of Intensity** for anaerobic workouts:

- **Rule #1.** Always build an aerobic base before introducing anaerobic workouts. The best way to determine that you have indeed built a strong base is steady improvement in MAF test results and generally feeling strong and energized from your training.
- **Rule #2.** Always be 100 percent physically energized and mentally refreshed when you conduct an anaerobic workout. Never force your body to do intense exercise when your spirit is not willing.
- **Rule #3.** Never conduct anaerobic exercise for more than six weeks without a break. Benefits will dwindle the longer you exercise intensely without a break. This is true even if you are observing rule #4 and limiting frequency of anaerobic workouts in your schedule.
- **Rule #4.** Limit anaerobic exercise to 10 percent of total weekly exercise time. Even during anaerobic training periods, time spent at high heart rates is only a fraction of total weekly exercise time.

Remember that during the anaerobic period, anaerobic workouts are your Key Workouts and all other workouts are characterized as "fill in the blanks." The top priority is to be 100 percent rested and motivated for your intense workouts. After six weeks of anaerobic exercise, you should introduce a micro-rest period of at least two weeks. During this period, you should cut back on workout time and frequency by at least 50 percent to ensure that you are totally rested when you resume training. During your anaerobic phase, total volume of training should drop sharply (at least 33 percent), and your basic standard fitness maintenance workout should drop, too. For example, if your standard swim workout is 3,500 meters, drop down to 2,000 to 2,500 during your anaerobic phase. If your standard run is 1:00, cut it back to :40 or less. Use your experience and life variables to determine what you can do while ensuring that you are rested and ready for the hard stuff.

"Okay, okay" you say, "I've met all the prerequisites and am ready to hammer. What kind of anaerobic workouts are the best?" The answer is: it doesn't matter that much. Coaches, books, and magazine writers spend much time and energy conjuring up the ideal anaerobic workouts—intervals, anaerobic threshold time trials, track workouts, hill repeats, 10K road races, and so on. The goal of anaerobic workouts is to prepare your body to handle what you will face in a race—a high-intensity effort where lactic acid must be processed effectively in the bloodstream so you can maintain as fast a pace as possible for as long as possible.

During the 2004 Outdoor Life Network Tour de France broadcast, Lance Armstrong's coach, Chris Carmichael, detailed the interval workouts he prescribed for Lance to prepare him for the 2004 Tour de France prologue. It is fascinating to learn how a champion like Lance prepares for peak performance, but the average viewer may want to look beyond the fancy technical graphs to understand where Lance gets his competitive edge.

It's like asking the world's best surfer for his favorite weight workout in the gym. Sure, it helps his competitive performance, but only because the brah has spent the past couple decades in the green room (surf vocabulary lesson: *green room* = when a rider is immersed in the hollow interior part of a wave. Also known as a tube ride or getting barreled). An aspiring surfer would benefit by learning the nuances of actually catching a wave in the ocean before worrying about what kind of weights to lift to prepare for the Pipeline Masters.

Any time you go fast and feel the burn, your workout contributes to your goal of race performance. If you can nail the Four Rules of Intensity, you can go pull an old tire on a rope up a sand dune for your anaerobic training and experience a training effect rivaling a customized workout delivered by the best running coaches and programs in the world.

You may be thinking the same thing that some guests at my lectures do, "Thanks Brad, that sounds great. Can you give me some specific workouts to do for my next race?" It's a sensible strategy to conduct workouts that approximate the challenge you will face in the race. For example, if you are preparing for my Auburn International half-iron distance race, you should consider sessions that reflect the competition distances and the hilly terrain of the Sierra foothills.

One of my favorite workouts for half-iron distance triathlon is an all-out 56-mile time trial on a course similar to the racecourse. This workout teaches your body to complete the exact competitive distance at a pace superior to your race pace (because you are not saving anything for the 13.1-mile run). The same example holds true for an Olympic distance racer doing a 40K time trial. With this workout under your belt you will feel comfortable and confident when you settle into your race day pace. A half-marathon road race at full effort is another excellent example, as are brick workouts that stack a bike and run together just like on race day. I favor bricks of a 10:1 bike-to-run ratio (bike 80, run 8 miles; bike 60, run 6 miles). For half-ironman preparation, brick with at least the bike race distance and consider going all the way up to 100-mile bike, 10-mile run.

A long-distance brick such as 100/10 can be conducted during the base-building period (you aren't going to do too well if you exceed aerobic heart rates on a 100/10 brick anyway). As the race date nears, I suggest shortening the length of your workouts and increasing your intensity. For example, a good Key Workout two months out from the race might be an aggressive pace 80-mile bike ride. One month out, the workout should evolve to the all-out 56-mile time trial.

Coming off of the base period and into fast-paced efforts can be a shock to the body. You can prepare your body for speed by throwing in some prelude sessions where you get leg/arm turnover or cadence going quickly without overstressing your system. This is accomplished by interval work of very short duration, followed by short rest. Because the work effort is so short, your heart always has a chance to recover before lactate accumulates in the bloodstream. These sessions should not be overly stressful; they should feel more like getting the kinks out before the serious stuff in the future.

As you transition out of the aerobic base period, here are some good workouts to prepare you for anaerobic training sessions.

- **Swim**: a series of 25-yard sprints followed by 25 yards of slow freestyle or alternate stroke. You will become accustomed to race pace and turnover rate.
- **Bike**: a series of accelerations lasting 1:00 to 1:30 with an equal rest period. It's nice to do these in the hills where your hard efforts can match the terrain. Punch it up a short steep hill or rolling section and coast downhill. You can vary the accelerations to sync with the terrain. The drill is to acquaint the legs with a little pain before you go into sustained, hard efforts in future workouts.
- **Run**: a set of "40/20s" lasting 10 minutes. This involves a brisk 40-second effort (at ≈5K race pace), followed immediately by a slow jog for 20 seconds. This develops leg turnover without stressing the heart too much due to frequent rest.

148

Do Bricks Mess with Your Chi?

More important than specific workout type is to have a positive attitude toward all of your workouts and enjoy conducting them. So choose the anaerobic workouts that are most appealing to you. I grew to despise the Masters swim sessions because there was too much rest in between sets; I'd always get cold, and my rhythm would be messed up by crowded lanes and passing slower swimmers. Instead I would go out into the Pacific Ocean and pick a distant landmark, swimming full speed toward my goal. There were no coaches recording my split times at lifeguard towers, but I guarantee you that these workouts benefited me more than when I was shivering in the pool, feeling anxious and frustrated with a workout that was not ideal for me. Regardless of the physiological differences in training effect, I enjoyed the ocean swim more and thus benefited more.

A woman I coach recently asked, "Do I have to do bricks? I hate bricks!" I can guarantee you one thing: if you hate a certain type of workout, it will compromise the benefits of the workout. Chinese Tao philosophy believes that we have three energies in our body: Chi, Shen, and Jing. Chi is your daily energy, something that fluctuates depending on whether you feel tired or energized. Shen is your radiant energy, what you project to the outside world. Someone with a lot of Chi will project a lot of Shen. Jing is your stored energy. We are born with a fixed amount of Jing; some people are naturally more energetic than others. Over the course of our lives, we steadily deplete our Jing.

If you break your will by pushing your body at the wrong times with workouts that you hate, you will deplete your Chi, your Shen, and also your Jing. The same is true if you are at a job you hate. You can get your Chi back by going to sleep early and taking a day off of training. However, if you engage in a repeated pattern of abuse or excessively stressful lifestyle practices, you will deplete your Jing— your precious stored battery juice. With Jing depleted, you accelerate the aging process and have a diminished potential to produce Chi or radiate Shen. In other words, if you don't like bricks, don't do them!

The Myth of Strength Training

Along the same lines as speed work, strength training obviously offers a quantifiable benefit to the endurance athlete. However, for the amount of energy expended during the workout, the benefits are minimal in comparison to more triathlon-specific workouts. Good times and proven benefits can be had from strength training and also from yoga, pilates, plyometrics, intervals, hill repeats, stretch cords, and long, slow overdistance. The question is not whether you will benefit from some form of physical training. The question is what is the best use of your time and energy if your goal is peak performance in triathlon.

If your goal is primarily to look sleek, slick, and tight and secondarily to perform well in triathlon, then strength training is a great component of a balanced cross-training, body-sculpting fitness program. If you have limited time and energy to expend on training, then you have to prioritize your workouts to what delivers the greatest benefit toward your highest goals. If your goal is to get faster as a triathlete, then your energy should be devoted to the most time-efficient training methods and workouts. In my opinion these are overdistance, aerobic workouts in the three events.

150

Put the buffest dudes in the weight room onto a racing bike and see how they compare in performance to Tyler Hamilton, the wispy 140-pound pro cycling star. Even in a four-minute all-out anaerobic sprint, they would be embarrassed. Lifting weights in the gym primarily makes you good at lifting weights in the gym. If you are training diligently in swimming, cycling, and running, then lifting weights in the gym can absolutely benefit your performance and recovery in these events. But it can also compromise performance and recovery. If your legs or your entire physical system are not fully recovered from a strength training workout while you perform a key endurance workout, your performance will suffer and so will the derived benefits of the workout. Remember the two rules are to rest for and recover from all Key Workouts.

Lance Armstrong may have discovered this when he introduced lower-body weight training for the first time in his career prior to the 2000 Sydney Olympics. He speculated that his weight training might have contributed to his admittedly "flat" performance (he won a bronze medal in the time trial after dominating all of the time trials in the Tour de France earlier that summer). Certainly there were many other variables (including the bike accident that resulted in a cracked vertebrae a month before the games), but the introduction of a new form of physical and muscular stress could have compromised peak performance—even for the greatest cyclist in the world.

Many of the athletes I coach like to argue the pros and cons of strength training with me: "I love strength training. I feel more balanced and energetic, and I think it really helps my triathloning." If that is the case, I believe that your intuitive sense of what kinds of workouts are enjoyable and effective win out over an argument presented by some author or coach or magazine article. I usually give athletes a free pass to go lift weights with the parting comment, "I hope someday that you are so tired from your Key Workouts that you don't feel like lifting weights!"

The Myth of Acclimatization

The simple premise of acclimatization is that if you are racing in a foreign or extreme environment, such as altitude, heat, humidity, or a distant time zone, you should arrive at your race destination early to get your body used to the new surroundings. This makes perfect sense, yet doing this can be a serious mistake for an athlete. The problem is that acclimatization itself is stressful to the body at a time when stress needs to be strictly minimized. Sure, it would be ideal to acclimate and be comfortable in race conditions, but it may be too difficult and stressful to pursue this goal before an important race.

Let's take a look at what happens when you try to acclimate in the typical manner. You train diligently all year for the Hawaii Ironman, but nothing can really approximate the surreal setting of the Kona coast, with its stifling heat, high winds, and barren mind-numbing landscape. Veterans say that when you get off the plane and get blasted with that hot wind, nothing can prevent you from freaking out at the concept that you are going to actually race all day in that weather.

So you decide to head to the islands a week or 10 days before the event to acclimate. You go through the arduous logistics of settling into your lodging, finding a place to get some good food, and finding suitable routes for training. As you adjust to these new variables, you also have to deal with recovery from jet travel and the elements of weather, terrain, and time zone. Then, after a week or more of struggling with the effects of a new environment, you finally start to feel better and get used to your surroundings.

But what is the cost of that struggle? Many athletes deplete their physical and psychic energy struggling to acclimate to a new environment before the race. I'm sure that you obtain many positive benefits from getting used to your competitive surroundings, but I believe they are outweighed by the additional stress. Oh, and I forgot to mention the impact of hanging out with a bunch of competitive athletes before your event. It's likely that your training will be disrupted in the excitement of mingling with a new group of athletes who are all fired up about the impending event.

The other alternative is to stay home as long as possible and fly to the race at the last moment. Many would be horrified at the thought of training all year for a big race and then waiting until the last minute to go there. This is not as easy as racing in your own backyard, but I believe it is much less physically and mentally stressful than arriving seven to ten days prior.

Take the example of altitude acclimatization. Conventional wisdom says that it takes three weeks for the physiological adaptation (increasing the density of oxygen-carrying red blood cells—the storied "altitude training effect") to take place in your body. Experts say that if you are racing at altitude, you should arrive either three weeks early to build more red blood cells or immediately before the event to avoid the stress of exercising, existing, and even sleeping at altitude. I would speculate that the same dynamic is true for a psychological acclimation. After three weeks, you are going to feel pretty comfortable and well adjusted wherever you are. After one day, you are certain to feel uncomfortable in new surroundings, but you can deal with anything for a few days without becoming exhausted by it.

"Hey, You Awake?"

My first international trip to compete in a professional event was the 1986 World Long Course Championships in Nice, France. We flew to France from Los Angeles, leaving in the morning and arriving the following French morning. Due to the nine-hour time change and the difficult trip, I was exhausted by midday and decided to take a short nap. Actually, I had no choice since my eyes refused to remain open. Some five hours later I woke up refreshed, went for a little jog along the famous Promenade des Anglais waterfront, and had a nice dinner. Boy getting over jet lag was easy!

What followed was a weeklong biorhythmical, jet lag nightmare. I was wide awake all night and an exhausted walking zombie all day. My travel companion Andrew MacNaughton and I had this joke every night where, lying awake and trying to nod off, one of us would whisper, "Hey, you awake?" "Yeah." Then we would flip on the light, fix a midnight snack, and watch weird late-night French TV—not exactly high on the priority list of an ideal prerace taper.

Then a funny thing happened on race morning after a fitful night of sleep: I woke up feeling energized and ready to race. Finally I had discovered a cure for jet lag—adrenaline! In future international travel I adopted a different strategy: I would fly to races at the latest possible time to minimize exposure to the new climate and time zone before my peak performance. I would pack a hot plate and suitcase full of food and cook my own meals in the room. (Hint: glass jars of spaghetti sauce don't always survive baggage handling. Other packed items, including garments, can be adversely affected.) Instead of fighting a flip-flop day, I would sleep liberally during the day and remain awake, reading or watching TV, at night. Who cares? I was there primarily to perform in the race, not be fresh and alert for a 10 A.M. museum tour. Adjusting to normal life and the local cuisine in some foreign land is not a prerequisite for hammering on race day. When the gun went off I was ready to race. Plus, when I returned home I had little trouble adjusting back to my normal clock.

The best place to prepare your body for peak performance is the comfort of your own home, familiar conditions, and terrain. If you live in the flatlands, don't expect to perform miraculously in a high-elevation race with lots of climbing. These are very formidable obstacles for the unfamiliar. But you can certainly expect to perform worse if you show up in the mountains a week before and try to grow new lungs or climbing legs. Yes, it will be a shock to discover how thin the air is during your competition, instead of having six training sessions to affirm how thin the air is prior to the race. You will in fact probably have to slow down when competing in a challenging environment. Train well, be healthy, arrive refreshed and energized, and give your best effort in whatever conditions you face.

Strategies to Acclimatize the Right Way

Do your best with what you have in your home environment. Athletes who live in Florida train for hilly events by doing repeats up waterway bridges—the closest thing to a hill for hundreds of miles. Olympic bronze medalist marathoner Deena Kastor lives and trains in the high-altitude community of Mammoth Lakes, California. Her goal event of the 2004 Olympic marathon was to be contested in the stifling heat and humidity of Athens, Greece. Even in midsummer, temperatures rarely exceed 80 degrees at the 7,800-foot elevation of Mammoth. To prepare for Athens, Kastor reported that she would run in full winter training gear to teach her body to deal with overheating. She devised training routes that mimicked the severe hills found at the end of the Athens route. Kastor believed that her preparation methods, coach, environment, training partners, and support system would help her prepare optimally for Athens. You could not pick a more dissimilar training environment between Mammoth and Athens, but being fit, healthy, and happy were bigger success factors for Kastor.

In contrast, Alberto Salazar took a different approach in preparing for the 1984 Olympic marathon, which was to be held on a hot summer afternoon in Los Angeles, California. At the time, Salazar was the number one–ranked marathoner in the world and one of the favorites to win a gold medal. Believing his Eugene, Oregon, training base to be too cool, he uprooted himself a few months before the Olympics and moved to Atlanta, Georgia, to train in more humid conditions there.

On race day in my hometown of L.A., I donned my ABC Television T-shirt and snuck into the athlete warm-up area. I had signed up to be an "athlete spotter" for ABC and was stationed at mile 16 of the course. I forgot about my post and used the shirt to gain access to the warm-up area and then to bust through the crowds at mile 6, mile 13, mile 18, and mile 25 as we raced across L.A. following the event.

I noticed that Salazar, looking visibly tense and nervous, had painstakingly shred his nice USA Olympic team uniform to provide more cooling. Then I watched another athlete: a 37-year-old oft-injured dark horse from Portugal named Carlos Lopes. Lopes had attempted only three marathons and finished just one prior to the Olympics. Furthermore, he was hit by a car 15 days before the marathon, sustaining minor injuries after rolling over the hood and crashing his elbow through the windshield. As I watched him warming up, our eyes met and he nodded to me. I said, "good luck, Carlos," and he smiled and gave me a thumbs-up.

A couple of hours later, Lopes was the first person to the finish line, running an incredible 2:09 in a race of attrition against the heat. The oldest Olympic marathon gold medalist in history was asked in an interview how he was able to outlast both the weather and the competition. He explained that he did not concern himself with the heat; he preferred to train in his temperate seaside home in Portugal and build his fitness to the highest level possible. He was not concerned about the car accident; instead he speculated that the accident had

How to Acclimatize Properly

• *Stay home.* Your first priority is to preserve your comfort by remaining in your familiar environment and familiar routine. Do your best to approximate the conditions you will face, as did Deena Kastor with her layers of clothing. Understand that your fitness level will always be a more significant performance variable than how familiar you are with the competition environment. If you are racing in the heat or high altitude, adjust your pace accordingly.

• *Make yourself at home, away from home.* When you arrive at your competitive venue, do everything you can to make yourself comfortable. Travel with your own food supply if food will be a challenge, and bring stimulating reading material or other diversions so you can enjoy your experience.

• *Don't get caught up.* Resist the temptation to get pulled away from your routine and competitive strategies when you are in a foreign environment. Countless athletes drift away from their routines in the presence of other athletes at a race site. If you normally relax the day before a race, don't be tempted by invitations from other athletes to "go spin an easy 20 miles."

• *Go with the flow.* Discard the macho, egotistical mentality that you must control and dominate every aspect of your environment. Respect unfamiliar and challenging conditions, and strive to make peace with them instead of battle them.

afforded him valuable extra rest. Salazar, however, finished 11th. The contrast between Lopes and Salazar in preparation and mind-set at the starting line proved striking in the result.

The suggestion to "go with the flow" can be interpreted as a water metaphor. Water experts like surfers, sailors, kayakers, or river guides respect the awesome power of water and make the essence of their activities to go with the flow. They use the power of the water to their advantage by accommodating it, ceding to it, or leveraging it—but never trying to overpower or disrespect it.

Similarly, you can face challenging environmental factors by altering your pace, training methods, and competitive strategy to go with the flow. You may even gain an advantage over your opponents who are not as clever, aware, or relaxed.

Mind Acclimatization

When we talk about acclimatization, we must discuss not only the physical environment but state of mind. It is important to make an effort to acclimate to the inevitable prerace nervous tension. Having a relaxed, positive mind-set before a race is ideal. Many athletes get keyed up and tense before races. While it's healthy to have some butterflies and anxiety before big races, I believe that many athletes drain their energy and diminish their potential with a negative mentality and destructive behavior before events.

Channel any tension, anxiety, or negativity that you feel into some type of positive thought or behavior. Whenever I felt tense, anxious, or negative before a race, I reminded myself that the opposite state of being would be boredom—not an attractive option. I was making a conscious choice to live an exciting life and pursue a goal that I had a passion for. I told myself that I should feel privileged to have the opportunity that I was nervous about facing. These thoughts did not instantly relax me, but they did put a positive spin on my nervous energy. This is an important goal to achieve before an event.

Prerace jitters are normal and healthy as long as you remain completely positive. Negative feelings or thoughts should be reframed into something positive and empowering. American pro James Bonney looks loose and ready to race!

CREDIT: ELIZABETH KREUTZ

During those final restless days and hours before the gun goes off, if you notice yourself snapping at your loved ones as an expression of your nervous energy, you need to get over yourself and get some perspective. A champion athlete is one who can control his or her emotions and behavior in the interest of peak performance. If you have trouble turning negative thoughts or energy into positive before the race, you sure as heck will have problems in the middle of a strenuous competition.

Today as a retired athlete I have an interesting perspective about prerace jitters. I feel excitement and even nervousness when I produce events and I get excited when I announce events, but nothing will ever compare to the feeling of standing on the starting line facing the challenge of a triathlon race. It's easy now to see what a rich, privileged experience it was to be able to race 130 triathlons on the professional circuit. My message to someone who has the good fortune and desire to race is to appreciate every moment of the experience—even the flat tires, the butterflies in your stomach, the heartbreaking defeats, and the peak performances. This is the best way to live life, and triathlon is a wonderful vehicle to experience this lesson in a powerful manner.

CHAPTER 8

SOLVING THE SWIMMING MYSTERY

Mastering Your Stroke

Let's dream for a moment about a new, wild, and wacky approach to swimming. Why not? Most triathletes have nothing to lose, based on their level of swim performance for the time invested. Maybe you have worked hard on your swimming with minimal improvement and maximum frustration, especially if you swim with Masters or age group teams and notice skinny 12-year-old girls or overweight ex–college swim jocks swimming circles around you. Maybe you are new to the sport and feel intimidated in open water or fall far behind the pace set by the superior swimmers in your age group. Almost all triathletes can benefit dramatically from challenging some of the generally accepted approaches to swimming and adopting a fresh, new approach to their swimming training.

One of the "gospel" theories of swim training is the importance of joining up with a U.S. Masters swim team. "Push yourself with faster swimmers and good coaching and you will certainly improve," is the party line you'll hear repeatedly. This may sound perfectly sensible and reasonable, but it is actually troubling. Masters workouts are great for ex–competitive swimmers who wish to maintain fitness and continue their competitive careers in the water. But many of the workouts (with the short intervals, mixed strokes, drills, and swimming aids) are designed to prepare athletes to compete in swim competitions that last a few minutes.

The swimming triathlete has specialized needs that are more difficult to address than just jumping into a lane at Masters a few times a week for a hammer session. First, you must understand that you are a triathlete, and swim workouts must integrate into your entire training schedule. Second, your swimming workouts should emphasize your performance goals. As the triathlon swim consists only of long-distance freestyle, your triathlon performance will benefit from workouts that emphasize distance and freestyle. Third, as discussed at length in the aerobic training section in Chapter 7, it is critical for an endurance swimmer to develop aerobic efficiency in the water. This is accomplished at comfortable heart rates, just like cycling and running. Only with a satisfactory base of aerobic swimming will you benefit from fast-paced swimming.

Fourth, and by far most important to the triathlete, is the development of efficient technique in the water. Because of the increased drag and resistance you face in the water, it is essential to swim with proper stroke technique. Good technique is exponentially more important to your performance than the yardage and interval sets that are the central element of most triathletes' swim training (and most Masters or other group workouts).

This point was driven home repeatedly for me and the group of accomplished triathletes I trained with in Los Angeles. Our coach, Jeff Thornton, won a dozen NCAA Division II national championships at Cal State Northridge, specializing in distance freestyle. He also got some TV time leading the swim at Hawaii Ironman one year in under 50 minutes. After several years of sedentary ways and carrying perhaps 75 extra pounds, he could still jump into the water with no

warm-up and pump out a few 200-yard freestyle efforts in 2:00. This was something he did every time we complained about a workout set or teased him about his sedentary ways—as in, "Let's see you try it, Coach!" His superior technique more than made up for several years of de-training.

Extensive swimming with poor technique will actually hinder your improvement. When you try to swim fast frequently, your stroke often breaks down under the stress of fighting to make an interval or swimming with fatigued muscles. High-volume, high-intensity swimming ingrains inefficient stroke patterns into your nervous system, making correction and improvement more difficult and bringing a high risk of burnout and even overuse injuries.

Swimming slowly while focusing on proper technique will ingrain proper technique into your nervous system. While you maintain proper technique, steadily increase your training pace and workout duration as your fitness improves. Get out of the pool when you notice fatigue causing your stroke to break down.

Mike Pigg's aerobic training story is an excellent example of applying this principle of shifting training emphasis from hard work to smart work in the water. With no competitive swimming background, Pigg was behind the eight ball from day one in his professional career as he faced a smattering of college All-American swimmers.

With his trademark work ethic, Pigg battled his way to adequate swim performances with a regimen of long, hard workouts in the pool. He was famous in Boulder for bravely entering the fast lane of the group workouts and barely surviving the interval times. While the elite swimmers would smoothly go through the sets, chatting on the lane lines for 15 seconds and then leaving for another steady 300-yard interval, Pigg would arrive at the wall just in time, heave a few high-altitude breaths and take off on another 300 with four seconds of rest.

After adopting the training principles of Dr. Phil Maffetone and emphasizing aerobic exercise in 1990 and 1991, Pigg changed his swimming regimen accordingly to de-emphasize hard intervals and build an aerobic base in the water. His typical workout? Six thousand yards of lap swimming by himself. Nothing strenuous, no intense sets in a highly competitive group workout—just long, comfortable strokes with devoted attention to proper technique.

An astonishing thing happened at the first pro race of the 1991 season, the America's Paradise Triathlon in St. Croix. Pigg exited the water on the feet of German Wolfgang Dittrich, one of the best swimmers in the history of the sport. The duo was two minutes clear of the elite first pack, a pack Pigg would commonly follow one to two minutes behind in previous years.

The pack of contenders got out onto the bike course and duked it out, all the while waiting for Pigg to make his trademark appearance and blow by them. But on this ride, he never came by. The group assumed that he had flatted and was out of contention. The field got a big surprise at the run turnaround when they saw Pigg charging toward them with a five-minute lead on his way to an easy victory!

These types of performance breakthroughs are very rare on the pro circuit. First of all, the elite-level athletes are all highly accomplished in each event, or they would not be able to compete at a high level. The weaknesses among the top athletes were generally accepted as unchangeable. Some people had difficulty in hot weather; some excelled better at short distance than long distance; the collegiate swimming stars were fixtures at the front of the line in the water but struggled throughout their careers to move their bulky bodies quickly on the run course. Conversely, the skinny runners struggled with swimming throughout their careers.

Even when I reached peak fitness levels, I knew I would never improve my swimming to the point where I could equal a competitor who swam at a national level for 16 years from age group through NCAA Division I competition. Similarly, someone who picked up running on the heels of a swimming background would have difficulty making up for the years and years of road mileage and intensive track competition that constituted my background. As highly competitive professionals striving to make a living at a very challenging sport, you learn to live with and make the best of your weaknesses—emphasize your weak spots in training and choose races that play to your strengths. A performance breakthrough is all the more amazing when you consider the caliber of athletes and their respective strengths in the pro field.

The Three Performance Variables in Swimming

In order to take a strategic approach to swim training and improvement for the triathlete, it is helpful to distinguish three performance variables for swimming success as follows:

1. **Stroke technique.** This is the most important by far. Improvement comes in leaps and bounds with simple corrections.

2. **Muscle endurance specific to the swim stroke.** This is where the swim yardage pays off, as does dry land training like the Vasa Trainer or Stretch Cordz.

3. **Cardiovascular fitness.** The triathlete is strong here from the accumulation of cardiovascular exercise in all sports.

Take an Olympic marathon runner and cross-country skier with a world-class aerobic system and stick them in the water. If their technique is poor or nonexistent, they will go very slowly if not drown. Without proper technique, all the muscular endurance and cardiovascular fitness is meaningless. I remember my shock when I first started training with an elite age group team and noticed the spindly 12-year-old girls matching my best efforts in the pool. They have excellent technique, muscular endurance for swimming, cardiovascular fitness, and arms the size of rulers.

The typical amateur triathlete scores an A or B in the muscular endurance and cardiovascular fitness categories and a D or F in swimming technique. Thus the ruler kid can out-split a good amateur by several minutes at Olympic distance or an eternity at an iron distance swim. It is difficult for people who begin serious swimming as adults to learn proper technique. Kids' nervous systems are more malleable than adults' for skills that require heavy kinesthetic awareness like swimming or a golf swing. For confirmation go to any driving range and witness all manner of chopping and butchering going on in the name of "swinging" a golf club. Adults simply have a hard time learning new skills.

To compound this problem, triathletes commonly pay little or no attention to learning or refining technique. They might do technique drills or even watch a video or read a book. These can all be helpful, but if you have an F grade in swim technique, and swim technique is the most important element of your swim training, you need massive intervention. Watching a video is a good start, but the ideal path to improvement would be to engage a qualified instructor in a series of intensive one-to-one stroke technique lessons.

In terms of return on investment, a monthly private swimming lesson is near the top of the list of all the triathlon expenditures, edging out that $3,000 average expenditure for a racing bike by a wide margin. Spend $1,500 on a good racing bike and the balance on swim lessons, massage therapy, chiropractic treatment, and the healthiest food, and you are way ahead of the pack before the gun goes off.

Most triathletes may have already heard this sage advice somewhere but feel a greater pull to hit the pool and pound out hard intervals with the group. The main benefit of these hard workouts is cardiovascular; swimming is a great exercise to work repeatedly at high intensity without the risk of fatigue and skeletal stress that come from running. Of course if you already have an A in the cardio class, swimming hard is like watering plants in a rain forest. It's an inefficient use of your training time and energy and can hamper any eventual attempts to correct stroke flaws.

While you also develop muscular endurance with intensive swimming, if you have poor technique this benefit will be severely compromised. Good distance swimmers with efficient body position and rotation will propel themselves primarily with the latissimus muscles (lats—on the side of the back), for they are the largest and most effective muscles for use in swimming. Check out the "wings" (massively overdeveloped lat muscles) on the guys and gals on the blocks at the Olympics for confirmation.

In contrast, swimmers with poor technique rely mainly on the forearms, biceps, triceps, and legs to propel themselves in the water. The poor swimmer must kick aggressively to maintain proper body position in the water. An aggressive kick in a distance swimmer is a sign of serious stroke flaws (body position drops because arms are "slipping" rather than pulling water during the stroke) and is an extremely inefficient use of energy. Working the large muscles of the lower body requires tremendous amounts of blood and energy and provides minimal forward propulsion. Try to kick 100 meters at high speed for confirmation—you will exhaust yourself quickly while moving very slowly. When the smaller muscles of the arms are emphasized (poor rotation and extension negate the powerful lats), you fatigue quickly, move slower than you should, and put unnecessary stress on the shoulder joints, leading to common overuse injuries.

It's All About the Feel

Proper freestyle technique involves moving still water throughout your stroke. You can actually feel this by standing in shallow water and slowly moving your hand through a proper "S" stroke pattern. Notice how if you move your hand backward in a straight line the water offers little resistance, while if you move in the S pattern of the swim stroke, you experience heavy resistance. When you move the arm straight back, you push water backward at the initiation of the stroke and then pass through a vacuum of water that is already moving backward for the remainder of the stroke. This is an example of "slipping" through the water. In physics terms, this is drag propulsion, as exemplified by a slow-moving paddleboat moving water in one plane directly backward. You move, but you move very slowly.

With the S pattern you impart lift propulsion and move as efficiently as possible. This is what a boat or airplane propeller does. From the initiation of your stroke to completion, you move water in different directions and thus always find still water to move. Rather than "slipping," you impart force onto a willing recipient (still water) and maximize your speed through the water.

Proper technique allows you to move fluidly through the water, which is known as having the "feel." Rip Esselstyn, one of the best triathlon swimmers in history and former University of Texas All-American swimmer, describes this feeling with his characteristic wide-eyed passion. "Over the course of my career, I have had numerous experiences in both swimming and cycling where I get what I call the 'feel.' It's a powerful, magical experience where my entire body is completely in sync with the rhythm of the activity, technique is perfect, and I literally feel effortless stroking through the water or pumping the pedals. The 'feel' is extremely elusive, but when it comes and you can lock into it, you don't even have to train. It's just there, you know it's there, and you know you are going to turn in a peak performance. It's actually frightening!"

While it is difficult to attach scientific relevance to Rip's enthusiastic claim, I believe he makes an important point. When you are able to relax and focus on smooth, efficient technique, your performance often becomes effortless. In Rip's case, his excitement and passion for discovering that zone of peak performance is a contributing factor to peak performance.

Rip was so consumed by finding the feel that he went to great lengths to re-create circumstances where the feel came to him. At the 1995 St. Croix triathlon, Rip began the cycling leg by quickly pedaling out of the transition area with his bare feet smashing his cycling shoes, which were already attached to the pedals. This is a common technique that pros use to save time. With shoes attached to cleats, you grab your bike, get your feet on top of the shoes, and start pedaling. Only when you attain a decent speed do you then reach down and slide your bare feet into the cycling shoes and fasten them. You do this one shoe at a time, pedaling in between to maintain speed and contact with contenders, and then carry on.

That day in St. Croix, Rip experienced the feel immediately on the bike—while his feet were still on top of the shoes. So, he decided to ride the entire 33 miles without reaching down to slip his feet into his shoes! He came off the bike second in an elite field—an outstanding performance by any measure but extraordinary considering he did not have the benefit of feet attached to pedals. Encouraged by his result, he took a knife to his shoes and cut most of the upper shoe last away, so that it would feel like his feet were on top of the shoe instead of inside them for future races. It's all about the feel.

Rip explained, "I think I've been able to figure out muscularly what's going on in the swim, bike, and run to effectively experience that effortless 'feel' in all three disciplines. In my most recent race [Rip is still competing at a high level at age 42]—a local duathlon in Austin, Texas—I completed the first run with over a one-minute lead on the field. In the previous three races of the series on the same course against the same competitors, I was between 1:30 and 3:00 minutes back after the first run. I knew I had the running 'feel' about a week before the race—and I still have it! I can't wait to see what happens in the next race!"

Maybe it sounds a little wacky to you, but consider that the source is an athlete who for nearly 20 years has engaged in minimal swim training but still turns in swim performances at the elite international

The unique and talented veteran pro triathlete Rip Esselstyn of Austin, Texas—forever in pursuit of the magical and elusive feel.

CREDIT: ELIZABETH KREUTZ

level. Rip has phenomenal stroke mechanics and feel for the water. These skills were honed over a long swimming career of intensive training and massive yardage, but the importance of technique is evident, with Rip still performing at an elite level on minimal training.

"Over the past 10 years, I have averaged 8,500 yards of swimming per week," says Rip. This is well below the typical elite triathlete putting in 20,000 to 25,000 yards a week. But what Rip concedes in actual training time, he makes up for in feel.

Overcoming Self-Limiting Beliefs

Early in my triathlon career, I formed self-limiting beliefs about swimming. I had a good reason—getting my butt kicked 25 times in a row by superior and more experienced swimmers. After a while, I started to think of myself as a poor swimmer and became intimidated on the starting line of races. After all, I was a skinny ex-college runner geek trying to battle it out with hulking, Gumby-like ex-college All-American swimmers. While it's true that I was inferior to the top swimmers, my attitude compounded my difficulties until I decided to do something about it.

I was inspired to make an attitude change and performance breakthrough by a couple of memorable experiences at the races. One was a brash offhanded quip from a fellow competitor, and the other was the sight of a delirious opponent collapsed at the finish line.

The quip came from the young, brash, and talented Australian Miles Stewart. As a teenager Miles was one of the top athletes in the sport at Olympic distance, a strong swimmer, and an excellent runner with an unparalleled finishing kick. He was a strategic cyclist— ideal for today's ITU events with drafting-legal cycling. In my career I had repeatedly suffered the misfortune of missing the pack in the swim and hence missing the pack on bike. A group of riders can put vast amounts of time on a solo chasing rider and decide the outcome before the run even starts.

On one occasion, I noticed a blatant disregard for nondrafting rules with a pack of riders ahead of me (heading back from the turnaround to which I was heading). Miles, the eventual winner, was in the pack. By the time I crossed the line, I was infuriated by the incident and the fact that the same dynamics had played out at my expense numerous times in the past. I accosted Miles, calling him a wheelsucker (sucking the air off someone else's bike wheel) and threatening to launch a formal protest. He let me vent for a while and then said in a thick, dismissive Aussie accent, "Ah Kearns, yah just pissed because ya can't swim fast enough to ride in the pack yourself."

I didn't really have a comeback to that one. Miles enlightened me to a deeper issue, the fact that a situation I believed to be out of my control could be looked at differently. The experience helped me to destroy and reframe self-limiting beliefs I had about swimming and about pack dynamics in the sport. Before, I would hope that I wouldn't get robbed by a pack of faster swimmers gaining an advantage on the bike (where I could otherwise catch and gain time on most of them with a level playing field). I discovered a better solution was to focus on my swimming performance and consider it the key to my success as an athlete.

While I did reorganize my training schedule to add a little more swimming and juggle some other sessions so I could be fresher for my swim workouts, the training modifications were secondary to my mentality changes. Psyched that I had discovered the secret to my success in the sport, I changed my perception to view the sport as a whole instead of three component parts. When I started my career, I was encouraged as much by my finishing place as by how my run splits stacked up favorably against the top pros. While this analysis brought silver linings to many race results, the segmentation of events turned out to be self-limiting.

In casual conversation, I frequently get the question, "Oh, a triathlete. What is your best sport of the three?" I would typically answer, "Well, I was a runner in college so that's my best event. I'm also strong on the bike, while swimming is my weakest." I decided to evolve to a different answer. When someone asked me what my best sport was, I started answering, "Triathlon." Then they would of course explain that they meant best of the three, and I would convince them and myself that there was only one sport, one event—a continuous swim, bike, and run competition. After all, when the gun goes off on race day the first person across the line is the winner. There are no breaks between events. ("Okay swimmers, great job. After you cross the line, please remove your wetsuits, dry off, and proceed to the transition area. The bike ride will start in 20 minutes.")

While I swam adequately and enjoyed good results during several periods in my career, the first time I made a real breakthrough in mentality was at the 1991 Bud Light US Triathlon Series event in Phoenix, Arizona. The previous month, at the season-opening race on the pro circuit in St. Petersburg, Florida, I had a terrible swim in very choppy water and spotted 1:30 to the leaders.

It was a very hot day and I flew through the run, passing nine guys on the course. I caught a glimpse of the only remaining guy ahead as I entered the final straightaway to the finish. He was zigzagging and barely made it across the line, 11 seconds ahead of me. He collapsed at the line and went straight to the medical tent for ice packs and an IV treatment. While a win is a win, and Thomas Huggins of South Carolina was the fastest guy that day, the impact of the homestretch drama was devastating. All I had to do was stay in the same area code in the water and I would have passed everyone by the four-mile mark of the run for an easy win.

The site of Thomas splayed out in the medical tent burned in my mind for a long time. I realized how precious 11 seconds is on the racecourse and how much time I was conceding in the swim with a self-limiting, nonaggressive attitude. I resolved that I would never again discount the importance of every second on the racecourse.

For the next race in Phoenix, I decided to play a little trick with my mind. As we assembled for the swim start, I pretended that I had flown to Phoenix for a 1,500-meter swimming time trial. I completely removed the bike and run from my mind. I stood on the shore, surveyed the swim course, and told myself, "this is it." I did everything I could to convince myself that the swim *was* it. For me, it was nearly true. One of the things I did on this path to destroy my self-limiting beliefs was to analyze past race results. Projecting a swim time in the main pack of the professionals (instead of actual, where I often fell behind the main pack), I discovered that I would have placed in the top three in nearly every single event I completed! If I could be competitive in the swim, the sport was there for the taking.

In my trance on the shoreline I noticed a peer on the circuit standing next to me, another guy who was great on land but notoriously weak in the water. I turned to him and said, "This is it—the swim is the key to our race. Let's get in there and kick some ass!" I then mus-

cled my way into the middle of the lineup, among the top swimmers
on the circuit. I think the other guy was left bewildered on the fringes
of the start pack, a place I inhabited for years.

When the positions sort out in the water in a competitive swim
field, it is crucial to "get on someone's feet"—follow as close as possible behind a swimmer ahead and benefit from swimming in the
slipstream created by his swim stroke. Similar to the air resistance in
cycling, swimming in water that is already disturbed by the swimmer
ahead allows for a much easier journey through the water, not to
mention assists with navigation and mentally maintaining contact
with other competitors.

When the inevitable jostling took place (two people fighting for one
person's prized feet), I typically ceded the battle, thereby saving energy
and the risk of getting my goggles whacked off my face. Instead, I
would simply wait for the rival to jump on the forward swimmer's
feet, then jump on his feet, becoming the third person in line. Well,
you can imagine what happens if you cede your position a few times.
The pack would hit a turn buoy and I would look up and discover I
was the last man in line. Even a slight escalation in pace can cause the
last man to drift outside the area of turbulent water and get dropped
by the pack. Once dropped, a pack that you were swimming comfortably in just a moment ago can quickly put 10, 20, or 40 seconds
on you.

The answer in swimming is to be aggressive. Paradoxically, this
comes naturally to a good swimmer and is very difficult for a poor
swimmer. The poor or underconfident swimmer starts on the sides of
the fray instead of right in the middle, repeatedly cedes his position
in the water, and sees himself falling behind again and again. Some
triathletes I coach who struggle with swimming report that their goal
in the water is to "relax, swim my own race, stay calm," etc. Instead
I counsel them to fight and be aggressive. Anyone who has done pack
cycling knows that the person who is not attentive and responsive to
pace escalations or strategic positioning gets quickly spit out the back

of the pack. You can't be polite in the water and expect to survive against tough competition.

In Phoenix, I exited amid the leading professional pack, in view of all of my main competitors. While I had exited with the pack many times before, this swim was a breakthrough because it was a triumph in mentality. I was the first person across the line that day, but I won an even bigger victory in my mind. I knew things would never be the same again in the swim. Sure, I was bound to get dropped again in the future, but not due to a lack of aggression or to self-limiting beliefs.

PART 3

DEVELOPING THE MIND OF A CHAMPION

CHAPTER 9

ENTERING THE ZONE AT WILL

In Part 1, I discussed my performances in the Palm Springs Desert Princess duathlons as examples of being in the "zone"—performing extraordinarily in competition while rising above the usual pressure, tension, and anxiety experienced at important races. I'm betting that every athlete can cite a personal example of a race or workout where he or she felt superhuman. Because they happen infrequently and often randomly, these performances seem mysterious and elusive. The truth is, you can enter the zone at will by learning how to take control of elements that you typically believe to be out of your control.

The significance of a workout, race, season, or career is what you make of it. Just like time, it's relative to the observer. This simple truth comes as a revelation to many self-absorbed athletes. It's cool to be competitive and care deeply about a passionate, compelling goal like athletic performance, but like the soccer hooligans who beat up referees when they think the refs cost their team the game, going overboard is not cool. Today I laugh, and sometimes even feel ashamed, about how caught up I was in my race results. I fought hard at races to place as highly as possible and give my best effort, which is honorable, but I did not always release attachment to the outcome.

Releasing your attachment to the outcome is the *only* way to truly relieve the pressure, tension, and anxiety that compromise peak performance. Peak performance comes when you enter the zone—relaxed, focused, confident, and totally in the moment for the duration of the event. When you are worried about your placing, time, competition, expectations of yourself and others, weather, and any other external variables, you instantly depart from the zone and reenter the rat race. Upon reentry, you can easily fall victim to negativity, ego demands, and the stressful, unhealthy influences that compromise peak performance and happiness.

When you are able to make a concerted effort to release your attachment to the outcome and remain positive and enlightened to the higher ideals of athletic performance or whatever else you are doing, you are on your way to entering the zone at will. Here are some tips to help you achieve this enlightened goal in your racing and in your life.

Choose a Positive Attitude

Viktor Frankel, Nazi concentration camp survivor and author of the classic *Man's Search for Meaning*, said, "The greatest human freedom is the freedom to choose one's attitude." You always have the ability and the freedom to choose a positive attitude. Imagine the superstar athlete who gets booed by 80,000 people and carries on with the usual focus and intensity. Imagine a professional cyclist, a world champion by the age of 23 and millionaire at 25, living the good life and suddenly being taken down with a swift and grave cancer diagnosis. In the span of a few hours, he goes from fighting for victory in the next race to fighting for his life.

You may recognize this premise as the true story of Lance Armstrong, as detailed in the number one bestselling autobiography *It's Not About the Bike*. Few people are more intensely positive than Lance. And few have had their resolve tested more severely than Lance did with his cancer diagnosis in 1996. I asked Lance about how attitude can help one face difficult circumstances. "It's critical to always remain positive, whether it's at work, racing a bike, or fighting an illness. Everyone walks and talks differently—you can have a relaxed, calm positive attitude or a very excitable, emotional positive attitude.

"In a life or death situation like my illness, I had no choice but to be positive. I had to believe in my doctors, my medicine, my treatment protocol, and in myself that I could beat it. I wasn't cynical at all, wasn't skeptical—I was absolutely convinced that I was going to get better."

I asked Lance if this was automatic or if it took some effort to stay positive. "It took a few days. My diagnosis [on October 2, 1996] was sudden, surprising, and quite serious. For a few days I was in shock—crying, scared, feeling great despair. Then as I went about the process of doing my research, I saw a glimpse of hope. I found the best doctors and the best place to get treatment and realized the possibility of recovery. After that it was automatic."

When you experience nerves at the starting line or adversity during the race, remember the power that you have to put a positive spin on everything that happens to you. In this manner, you can take control of things that are seemingly out of your control. The Johnny G quote, "Turn adversity into opportunity," can actually become words for you to live by rather than a platitude to read in a book. If you get caught in a rainstorm during a training ride and get three flat tires trying to get back home, you can curse your bad luck or you can remember what a privilege it is to be outdoors experiencing weather.

I witnessed a question-and-answer session where Lance was asked whether inclement weather compromised his race preparation or his

The intensely positive Lance Armstrong. Nothing gets in his way of success. While others may fret about the weather, Lance says, "When it's raining, I just put on a rain jacket and go."

CREDIT: WILLIE J. STAPLETON

attitude. His answer: "Nah. When it's raining, I just put on a rain jacket and go." I doubt Lance grasped the significance of his casual, knee-jerk answer at that moment. For most people, it's not easy to just put on a rain jacket and go. Every day we face some form of inclement weather in our lives. The people who can face it with a positive attitude are the ones who win.

At this point you can drill down and investigate the core of what you really need to be a peak performer. Dig deep through the pile of magazine ads for fancy new equipment, through all the temptations of ego-boosting instant-gratification competitive workouts, through all the vanity and superficial recognition for your ripped physique and your age group podium finish, and ask yourself if you have what it takes to choose a positive attitude at all times.

As you proceed with this new awareness, catch yourself when you start to drift. When that figurative inclement weather arrives, do you put on a rain jacket and go? Or do you complain, explain, ponder, and blame? Do you choose the right garment for the situation or spin your wheels working really hard but not smart? Do you wear short sleeves into the rainstorm and return hypothermic again and again? Or do you learn from your mistakes and face the same challenges better prepared in the future?

Lance explained how cycling helps him face challenges in other areas of his life and improve as a person. "I prepared for my treatment like it was a bike race. I made cancer like an opponent that I hated and wanted to beat very badly. I believe the athletic approach, the athletic mentality, was very beneficial. I did everything with 100 percent efficiency, just as you must do to peak for a championship race. My research, understanding the drugs and the treatment protocol, taking care of my body, eating a healthy diet—I went 100 percent on everything."

I was reminded of just how intensely positive Lance is during an encounter several months after he shared those comments with me. It was at his annual "Ride for the Roses" gathering in Austin, Texas— a gala weekend of festivities to raise money and awareness for his Lance Armstrong Foundation cancer charity.

I was at a small cocktail gathering and Lance was signing a stack of posters for me to give to VIPs at the company I worked for. On that spring afternoon, he was plagued by allergies and was sneezing repeatedly (not on the posters, though). I made a comment about the thick, muggy spring weather in Austin, lamenting the difficulty of training and even living in that kind of weather. He looked up from his posters, right into my eyes, and said, "Quit bitching."

I was taken aback at the time because, after all, this was just some typical weather small talk at a cocktail gathering. I could have passed the comment off as Lance being Lance, but a deeper insight occurred to me upon reflection on that interchange. I thought, "How dare I complain about the weather to a cancer survivor at a gathering of cancer survivors!" Lance's comment woke me up to how routine it is to complain and lament our lot in life. When you want to conduct yourself like a champion, even idle chitchat about the weather may need to be examined and reframed.

Enjoy the Movie

Consider living your life as if you were watching a great movie. You experience all the emotional highs and lows, shed tears of sadness and tears of joy. But when the movie is over, you leave the theater and go on with your life. Every day is a new movie to be enjoyed and appreciated, regardless of the outcome.

184

Remember Your True Purpose

Write a note confirming your commitment to a pure and natural approach and post it in a prominent place. Give yourself tangible, visual reminders to stay on the right path. For example, you could write a message like: "I exercise to challenge myself physically, experience a healthy lifestyle, and learn and grow as a person. I strive for results but release my attachment to the outcome."

This will help you develop the ability to become positive and light-hearted about your athletic efforts. This is your key to entering the zone at will. Rip Esselstyn can tap into his mystical "feel" where hard exercise becomes effortless because he has an unfailing and intensely positive attitude, loves the sport, and loves the activity and the pure joy of moving his body through water, on land, or astride a bicycle. The feel and the zone are within your reach. You just have to let go of the stress of attachment and the ideal of suffering that plague those who have rat race mentality.

No Worries, Mate

At a 1993 ITU World Cup series race in the French Alps, an Australian professional named Chipmunk Slater was at the head of the field when he lost control of his bike on a steep descent and essentially flew off the edge of a cliff. He was out of the race but luckily not critically injured. I heard about the accident and saw him later that evening in the athletes' compound. Grotesque open wounds covered his face, and some of his teeth were missing and chipped (no doubt enhancing the future power of his nickname), yet he smiled and joked with the other athletes, lightheartedly rehashing his harrowing experience.

Slater had no trouble accepting the fact that going from one moment dreaming of a $5,000 payday to crashing and peeling the skin off his face was an occupational hazard of the professional triathlete. I've faced six-foot surf and violent riptides in Huntington Beach, the 55-mile-per-hour winds of 1986's tropical storm number 10 in Fort Lauderdale, and the famous Mark Allen race-morning stare in Australia, and none were able to intimidate me. But seeing Slater smiling through his asphalt exfoliant treatment had me pondering retirement! His disposition gave me a glimpse of a commitment level higher than I could even imagine. Slater provided a great example of the carefree "no worries, mate" mentality that is embodied by many Australian athletes. It's no wonder they dominate the sport and have so much fun doing it.

I am not suggesting that the secret to success is to devote yourself to the sport at the level of an elite athlete, taking life- and face-endangering risks on mountain roads in the French Alps. However, when you take some time to reflect on your purpose for competing in triathlon, you will benefit greatly.

In my case the end of my career came in the final mile of the Wildflower half-iron distance race in 1995. I had run comfortably in second place for the entire run and was descending a steep hill to the finish line when I heard the unpleasant sound of heavy breathing from behind. I glanced back to see a wild-eyed rookie professional recklessly slamming his quads into the pavement in a mad dash to the finish line. For the previous nine years, that had been me: someone who would fight to the death when in contention for money and the honor of a top finish. A few thousand dollars of prize and bonus money were at stake trading a second place for a third, but I let the guy go without even a minor effort or a second thought.

At that moment, before I even crossed the finish line, I knew I was done. If you have a clouded or conflicted purpose as a professional athlete, you are a living, breathing example of self-inflicted failure. Professional sports, like many other intense avocations, is a do-or-die proposition. You don't see emergency room nurses or airplane pilots showing up for work dreaming about a different job or performing their duties half-assed.

Both professional and amateur triathletes need to give 100 percent effort and commitment to achieve success in the sport. Whatever happens, you can go back to work Monday morning and still receive a paycheck, and family and other real-life responsibilities may take precedence over your workout schedule. However, when it's time to be an athlete, the most rewarding choice is total commitment. It is a gift to be able to pursue triathlon and, as the late, legendary distance runner Steve Prefontaine said, "To give anything less than your best is to sacrifice the gift."

Commitment to doing the sport correctly means disciplining yourself to follow your intuition and make the best decisions in training. It means controlling your ego, emotions, and self-limiting beliefs to give yourself a fighting chance at peak performance on race day. Get clear about your purpose for pursuing triathlon, and live in accordance with that every day at every workout and every race that you do.

CHAPTER 10

HELP YOURSELF TO PEAK PERFORMANCE

Snap Your Fingers

I've read plenty of self-help books, but lately I have become stuck. The problem is, even if the books are written by good authors and have compelling messages, I feel like I already have enough information in my brain. The fact that I still do not live an ideal life is not going to be solved by another book. The problem comes not from lack of knowledge but from something else that is harder to quantify. All triathletes know that rest is a good idea when the body is tired, but quite often behavior is not in alignment with this ideal.

The best chance for success in behavior change comes when you start with a clean slate, a positive attitude, a plan of action, and—most important—a natural approach with a pure motivation. When you have this foundation, it is easy to align your behavior with your goals, values, and ideals.

I have worked with many people who have failed with weight-loss efforts. A common mind-set they share is negativity, which sets them up for failure again and again. There is little motivation to eat healthy foods or enjoy food as one of life's great pleasures if your happiness is dependent upon a number on a scale. As Dr. Andrew Weil said in his bestseller *Eating Well for Optimum Health*, the term "eating well" means more than just eating nutritious foods; it means enjoying the entire experience of eating. People who are motivated simply to eat well have a great chance at reaching the superficial goals that are so elusive to millions of dieters.

Similarly, if you are motivated as an athlete by anger, a fragile ego, or emotional voids like lack of respect, inner peace, validation, or recognition, you may have natural and pure ideals in your head but behave like a fool. The person who is focused on a superficial goal will find motivation destroyed if everything does not go according to plan. And when everything does go according to plan and success is attained, that person may experience an empty feeling rather than the bliss that comes with behaving in alignment with your ideals.

Whether your goal is weight loss, financial management, or athletic performance, a positive attitude is mandatory for any true progress to be made. Yes, those with bad attitudes have won big races and built huge companies, but success should be defined more deeply than by superficial results. Often these "winners" don't seem happy, balanced, or healthy, despite their triumphs. I don't know what it feels like to be filthy rich or to have an Olympic medal, but I know it's not worth sacrificing my happiness or morality.

When triathletes overtrain or self-sabotage, they replay certain thoughts: "This guy is so annoying, I have to drop him on this 'recovery' workout; I swam so poorly in the last race I need to double my yardage; this injury can't stop my running now—the race is six weeks away." We know better but we are clever enough to convince ourselves otherwise. Deep down, however, it is hard to fool the face in the mirror. You know when you lie to yourself and behave incongruently. You may even feel guilty about it.

Consider right now as the time to snap your fingers and resolve to do something different going forward. Accept your shortcomings, compulsions, and human frailties as necessary components on your path through life. Understand that your past behavior served an important purpose to get you to this point; now you can choose to discard that behavior as you continue to learn and grow. Join the many inspirational examples of people who have experienced tragedies or setbacks and choose to move on, taking something positive with them about their past experience.

Whoever you are, regardless of how much extra weight you are carrying or how flawed your swim stroke is, you can become a champion triathlete. I don't mean winning your division or making the national team—I mean giving your best effort and experiencing peak performance. Or as Lance would say, "doing the sport correctly." To be great in anything you have to take risks. It is a huge risk, a leap of faith, to leave past beliefs, attitudes, and behavior patterns behind in favor of an enlightened approach.

You have all the tools and knowledge you need; you just have to make a commitment to a new way. Commitment means you make a decision, set a goal, and do whatever it takes to succeed. To most of us this means getting somewhere, like crossing a finish line, closing a deal, graduating from college, or losing 10 pounds. Commitments like these are fluff compared to a way of life commitment. When you commit to a process instead of an end result, that's when you can experience what it's like to be a great triathlete. In the meantime, results take care of themselves. Results happen naturally when motivation is pure.

When It Rains, It Pours

Craig Eigenbrod, a friend and competitive Masters cyclist from Indiana whom I coach, demonstrated a dramatic example of commitment at the 2004 Race Across INdiana (RAIN). This unique event traverses the entire state of Indiana, starting at the Illinois border and

Six-time Hawaii Ironman champion Natascha Badmann of Switzerland exudes an enlightened attitude toward the sport. "I got into triathlon to become a happy and healthy person. I want to do it for the rest of my life. Ironman is something that teaches you so much about yourself."

CREDIT: ELIZABETH KREUTZ

ending 158 miles later at the Ohio border. In the 2003 event, he finished ninth in a field sprint. It was a respectable result, but Craig wanted more in 2004. He trained diligently throughout the spring and early summer for the July 2004 event, often riding 20 to 40 extra miles on top of organized 100-mile "century" events to prepare his body for the race distance.

The week of the race, we discussed strategy. As Craig carried on about the possible scenarios and how he and his team would react, a thought occurred to me. It was a thought aligned with my message of taking risks, giving 100 percent effort, and enjoying the process. I posed the idea to Craig that he launch a breakaway immediately after the race begins (on the outskirts of a town after a controlled-pace police escort over the first 10 miles). He thought I was kidding. I told him that he was strong, that he had a great team devoted to work for him, and that a "crazy" move like this would ensure that he deliver full effort and receive full satisfaction from his effort. Craig cautiously brought it up at the team meeting a couple of days before the race, and the group decided to go for it.

Well, the breakaway worked and by halfway Craig and a teammate were 12 minutes clear of the field! Craig broke the tape in his dream race, teammate Bryan Boggs (national champ age group triathlete) in tow, three minutes ahead of the 892 cyclists who had chased him with increasing ferocity for nearly seven hours. It was a performance beyond his wildest dreams. It became a reality because Craig dared to challenge his self-limiting beliefs about the possibility of a suicide breakaway, challenge the stagnant nature of tactical cycling (where everyone waits for everyone else to make a move), and look beyond an obsession with results to an enjoyment of the process.

This is a dramatic illustration of a lesson we can all experience every time we compete or challenge ourselves in any way. When facing a challenge, it is human nature to start rolling the tape of self-limiting beliefs. I was amused to notice young children at my son's elementary school verbalizing self-doubt about their ability to perform well in an informal distance-running competition I conducted at the school. By first or second grade, children are already accustomed to being measured and judged by their performance and developing protective mechanisms against the perceived failure of not measuring up. It is this type of thinking and behavior that can be overcome with the snap of the fingers—like the moment when Craig accelerated out of the pack at the beginning of the 158-mile RAIN, knowing there was no turning back.

Yo, Adrian

Believe it or not, I think movie stars are good examples of people with pure motivation and commitment to the process. Anyone familiar with moviemaking knows it's an incredible grind: long days of sitting around the set, hurrying up and then waiting to perform dozens of takes of the same scene, and striving for perfection. It's not the least bit glamorous; the fans and parties are missing during those four-month shoots on location in Mississippi or Borneo or wherever. For the big stars, moviemaking isn't even about the money, for they already have more money than they can ever spend. In fact, it's common for A-list actors to work for scale (actor minimum wage of $695 per day) if they feel passionate about a low-budget project.

Actors are inspired by the process of creating art, even if the process requires 27 takes to film the same scene. Sure, the end result brings the superficial rewards of fame and wealth, just like when you bask in the cheers at the finish line after thousands of miles of anonymous hard training. But even though many get caught up in the excess and fluff of being a celebrity, that's usually not the reason they choose to be actors. The odds against becoming a celebrity are too overwhelming for any rational person to pursue acting for superficial reasons.

In Sly Stallone's early Hollywood days, he was just another struggling actor slumming for roles in soft-core B movies. Inspired by a real Muhammad Ali versus longshot Chuck Wepner title fight, Stallone wrote his *Rocky* screenplay in three days. He pitched it around town with himself in the lead role. With $106 in his bank account, he passed on a whopping $300,000 offer from a studio that wanted the script but with Ryan O'Neal in the lead. When Sly refused to budge on his package offer, the project was finally green-lighted with a tiny ($1.1 million) budget. The result was a 1976 Best Picture Academy Award and eight other nominations, including Stallone for best actor and best screenplay.

There is an analogy here for triathletes. Just like acting, the sport is too difficult to do just for superficial reasons. Deep down, everyone has a pure motivation for participating. Stallone believed that *he* was Rocky and nothing could compromise his pure motivation for bringing the character to life. The pure and natural side of an athlete battles the superficial pulls of the rat race, which lead to confusion and disappointment. The message of this book is not to add more stuff but to let go of some things and allow the healthy, natural, pure elements of your athletic experience rise to the surface. And when they do, you enjoy profound rewards from pursuing a crazy sport like triathlon. These rewards carry over into all facets of your life.

Roger Bannister conveyed this concept perfectly at the end of *The Four-Minute Mile*, so I will leave you with his words:

> We run, not because we think it is doing us good, but because we enjoy it and cannot help ourselves. It also does us good because it helps us to do other things better. It gives a man or woman a chance to bring out the power that might otherwise remain locked away inside. The urge to struggle lies latent in everyone. The more restricted our society and work become, the more necessary it will be to find some outlet for this craving for freedom. The human spirit is indomitable.

INDEX